Life of Theobald Wolfe Tone

Alice L. Milligan

Copyright © BiblioLife, LLC

This historical reproduction is part of a unique project that provides opportunities for readers, educators and researchers by bringing hard-to-find original publications back into print at reasonable prices. Because this and other works are culturally important, we have made them available as part of our commitment to protecting, preserving and promoting the world's literature. These books are in the "public domain" and were digitized and made available in cooperation with libraries, archives, and open source initiatives around the world dedicated to this important mission.

We believe that when we undertake the difficult task of re-creating these works as attractive, readable and affordable books, we further the goal of sharing these works with a global audience, and preserving a vanishing wealth of human knowledge.

Many historical books were originally published in small fonts, which can make them very difficult to read. Accordingly, in order to improve the reading experience of these books, we have created "enlarged print" versions of our books. Because of font size variation in the original books, some of these may not technically qualify as "large print" books, as that term is generally defined; however, we believe these versions provide an overall improved reading experience for many.

LIFE

OF

Theobald Wolfe Tone

BY

ALICE L. MILLIGAN.

*Published at the Office of the "Shan Van Vocht,"
65, Great George's Street.*

BELFAST:
Printed by J. W. BOYD, 5, 7 & 9, Academy Street.
1898.

To

Miss KATE A. MAXWELL,

Of Brooklyn, New York, U.S.A.,

Great Grand-Daughter of

Theobald Wolfe Tone,

This sketch of his life is dedicated by the Author.

" Béidh Ulanh fós gan bhrón
Ag cuimhniughadh ar Wolfe Tóne."

PREFACE.

IRELAND in olden times was a free and highly civilised country. It had local government and Imperial Government; a judicial system of a very satisfactory nature; educational advantages sufficient to attract princes and scholars from other countries to it as a seat of learning. Enlarging her influence beyond her own island borders, she had sent forth invasions, and had settled colonies in the adjacent island now called Great Britain. She had done greater service to the world by sending forth apostles to Christianise Western Europe, and by stemming the tide of Paganism which swept in with the Danish invasions up till the tenth century. In the twelfth century, weakened by the dissensions which existed between her great Royal houses, the O'Neills and O'Briens, Ireland herself became the prey of the invader. Since that time she has been struggling in the grasp of England—never quieting into perfect submission, never quite breaking free. With the exile and death of Hugh O'Neill and his sons, Ireland's dream of a native Royal dynasty faded. The coming of Owen Roe and his career of victory revived it; but when women caoined around his corpse in the Lake Castle of Cavan on that sad St. Leonard's Day they wailed the dirge of the last native chief who might have been King of Ireland.

The wars in Ireland after this were on behalf of the Stuarts. For "Righ Shemus," the Catholic King, whose rule would have meant freedom to exercise their faith, Irish blood was freely spilt at Aughrim and the Boyne, before the Walls of Derry and behind those of Limerick; and though he proved all unworthy, Irish fidelity still did homage to him and to his son and grandson in exile, and the bards of the Gael sang sweet songs about the Royal blackbird and the princely lover of Kathleen ny Houlahaun. On Culloden Moor the doom of the House of Stuart was sealed, and the Gaelic bards changed their joyful chants to songs of sorrow. The middle of the eighteenth century was her time of blackest trouble. She had no king, no deliverer to dream of. And yet methinks even in that dark time the children of the Gael never bowed to the conqueror. It was then that there grew in their hearts that wholesome bitter hatred, born of resentment against intolerable injustice and utter scorn of the tyrant. Then, when Ireland was trampled lowest, she rose highest in the sight of God, refusing to sell her birthright. England had decreed that one form of worship should be tolerated in her dominions, and from the days of Elizabeth onward to refuse to accept the forms of the English Church meant to forfeit all worldly advantages. The Irish people willingly sacrificed all and kept their chosen faith, and in so doing they preserved also the spirit of freedom. The native Catholic Gaels in their struggles against religious persecution found allies in good time amongst the descendants of those very colonists whose courage had been the bulwark of English supremacy in this country during the Confederation and later, and more notably during the Williamite wars. The penal code did not spare the staunch Presbyterians of Ulster. The very men who had fought on Derry Walls for civil and religious liberty found all too late that they had been fastening shackles to their own limbs. In the early part of the 18th century there was an exodus of the Presbyterians of Ulster to the land of promise beyond the Atlantic, and in the War of Independence, which transformed the American Colonies into a free Republic, these Irish exiles helped to avenge the wrongs of that Ulster Colony from which England's bigotry had driven them.

The spirit of revolt awoke in the hearts of the Presbyterians who remained behind. In 1782 an Ulster Presbyterian Church was the scene of that armed gathering of the Volunteers, which dismayed England into recognising the independence of the Irish Parliament. From that time forward, even though the Volunteers were disbanded, the arms they had wielded were not laid aside nor forgotten. The wrongs of the oppressed Catholics, the wrongs of the insulted Presbyterians, set them thinking not of reform, but of Freedom. The foundation of the American Republic set before their eyes a new ideal—one which the courage of Irish exiles across the Atlantic had helped to achieve, and which the courage and sacrifices of Irishmen at home might avail to realise. But Ireland was weakened by disunion; Catholics and Presbyterians, groaning under the same tyranny, held apart in different camps, and worked even when working to one end in separate organisations. A Union of all elements hostile to English tyranny could alone make Ireland strong enough to strike against it.

In the present day the principles of the United Irishmen seem natural and easy of acceptance; but in the last century they were a revelation.

Remember that the great National wars of Ireland had hitherto aimed at the expulsion of the colonial element and the restoration of all lands and governing powers to the native Catholic Gaels. The

PREFACE. 5

Penal Laws might have been expected to force the people of Ireland into all the frenzied ardour of a war for the faith. If these afflicted, down-trodden children of the Gael had risen in fury and hate to massacre and extirpate everyone in this country not Catholic and Irish, the world, knowing the story of their wrongs, could not have greatly blamed them.

But in that century of sorrow the down-trodden Gaels had learned lessons of wisdom and tolerance. They saw the hatefulness of tyranny; they learned by their own experience that religion should not be promulgated by force of arms, or fires of persecution. When they armed and took the field they did so not merely as champions of their faith, but for the principle of civil and religious liberty, scarcely, or at all, recognised by the Governments of the world in that day, and not recognised by the so-called civilised English Government for many a long year after the swords of the United Irishmen had rusted in the dust. They linked with the cause of Catholic Emancipation and Irish Independence the principles of complete religious toleration, and no Irish National movement has since that time retreated an inch from the lines marked down in '98. England has again and again cunningly tried to introduce the dividing lines of sectarianism, and to entangle Irish Nationalists on one side or the other. She is doing so in this very year, but we have faith in the spirit of Young Ireland, which is turning its face towards the graves of '98. The memories which will be awakened will save us from falling a prey to England's insidious policy, well summed up in the *dictum*—" DIVIDE AND CONQUER."

Theobald Wolfe Tone devoted his life to promoting *Union* among Irishmen. This fact has been sufficiently emphasised by politicians of various parties since the dawning of this centenary year, 1898. Unity has become, in fact, one of the watchwords of the day, and we take it up and echo it—but with a difference. Tone preached Union not for the sake of peace, or quietness, nor even for the sake of appearances! His aim was not Unity, but Freedom. He did not concern himself with the differences which existed among political parties in his own day, nor did he exert himself to allay them. He was not a reformer, but a revolutionist. He aimed not at mending Grattan's Parliament, but at overthrowing its authority He sought not justice from England, but a foreign ally for Ireland, and he found one in the Republic of France. The story of his life-work has been written by himself and published early in this century by a son who inherited his patriotism and talents. To that priceless work we would point any reader who has access to the libraries of Belfast, Dublin, or Cork. The main substance of this life has been recently republished in two volumes by Fisher Unwin, of London, edited by R. Barry O'Brien. These volumes should be on the book shelves of every patriotic Irishman who is in a position to pretend to anything in the form of a library. In Madden's *United Irishmen* the most minute biographical details are given regarding Tone's comrades and fellow-workers. In Fitzpatrick's *Secret Service Under Pitt* you get a revelation of the counter-conspiracy of spies and informers by which they were entangled. If you will understand the tyranny that Ireland groaned under and which Tone swore to save her from, go to the pages of Mr. Lecky's History dealing with Ireland in the 18th century.

This little volume is written for the benefit of that numerous class of people in Ireland who cannot afford the luxury of expensive books, and who have not access to libraries. It may also perchance fall into the hands of persons of education and culture ignorant of their country's history. We have met with graduates at Trinity College (Tone's own Alma Mater) who knew nothing of him, and men of culture and intelligence in Belfast unaware of his connection with that town. In the short space at our disposal no adequate account of Tone's political work in Ireland was possible; we have, therefore, dwelt at greater length on the narrative of his negotiations with France, and the story of his arrest, death, and trial.

We publish a description of his last resting-place at Bodenstown from the pen of Michael Cavanagh, of Washington, the sole survivor of the deputation sent from America to Ireland with the coffin of Terence Bellew MacManus. The facts regarding the graves of Tone's wife and son come to us from the grand-daughter of the latter, Miss Kate Maxwell, of New York. We owe our introduction to this lady to Mrs. John Martin, sister of the patriot, John Mitchel, the man, above all others, who in this century has given living proof that the principles of the United Irishmen were not dead in Ulster. Thank God we have not to look back a hundred years for examples of defiant, unswerving patriotism. Our own century, with all its sorrows and defeats, has been fertile in examples of devotion to the undying cause, and now when many are lamenting the political disasters and dissensions of the past few years it seems to the present writer that we are entering upon an era of great hope. English misrule has almost passed away; it might be supposed that now, if ever, Ireland would settle down contentedly as a province. Are there any signs that she will do so? By no means? Now that reform has gone as far as needs be, the fact remains plain, that Ire-

PREFACE.

land has an ideal which no mere reform can replace. The ardent youth of Ireland, uncrushed by any disappointment, unallured by any golden bribe, have gone even further than Wolfe Tone in their aims for Ireland. They dream of restoring to their place among the Nations *the race of the Gael*. This ideal was preached by Thomas Davis and some of the scholarly young Irelanders. John O'Mahony upheld it when he revived the name and memory of the *Fianna Eirinn*. For many years it seemed lost sight of by our public men, but now the Gaelic revival is becoming the talk of the literary world; the Sassenach is by no means alarmed, is even pleased and interested by the novelty of the thing. Some day, please God, the Clans of the Gael shall make history as well as literature. The Sassenach will scarcely like that quite so well. Even as we write, the gossiping wires of the world are thrilled with rumours of an alliance of the Teutonic nations. Truly we do not mislike the idea. If it becomes a reality, perhaps it will help Irishmen across the Atlantic to decide that

IRELAND IS THEIR COUNTRY,

and to remember, moreover, that the Gaelic race survives outside of Ireland in the country which in '98 numbered among its soldiers the subject of this memoir—Theobald Wolfe Tone.

Life of Theobald Wolfe Tone.

Chapter I.

BIRTH AND PARENTAGE.

N the 20th day of June, 1763, there was born in the home of a coachbuilder in Stafford Street, Dublin, the first child, a son, who was destined to bring joy and pride and tragic sorrow into the lives of his parents, and whose name has become, we may now assert, world-famous and immortal. The life that commenced on that midsummer day was one which was to be devoted unselfishly to the saving of the country in which the first heart-beats thrilled, the first breath was drawn. In that hour of darkness, when many deemed that the beacon fire of Freedom had for ever dwindled into nothingness, here like a tiny kindling spark was a soul awakening that ere long would fire it into a living blaze, flaring forth the signal that swords were yet to be unbared in Erin. Peter Tone, the father of this boy, was the son of a County Kildare farmer; his wife, who was the daughter of a sea captain called Lamport, had been till the time of her marriage a Catholic, and at the end of her life returned to that faith; but all her children were brought up in their father's creed. Through this mother,

Theobald Wolfe Tone and all his brothers inherited the sea-roving, adventurous disposition of sea-captain Lamport; from her also they doubtless learned to hate the system of penal persecution by which England was oppressing her Catholic kindred. Tone in his autobiography states that his parents were much like other people, but adds that every single member of the family was in some way remarkable, and, indeed, from the time this restless batch of boys began to run about Peter Tone and his wife must have had an anxious time of it. They were destined to outlive them all; to see two of them, Matthew and Theobald, die for their country; two others William (the second son) and the youngest, Arthur, after careers of varied adventure, the former in India, the latter at sea, were to mysteriously disappear, leaving no trace. The one girl of the home, Mary, who shared her brother Theobald's wanderings, was to be lost just as unaccountably in a Negro rising in Jamaica. Truly enough of incident in the lives of one Irish family. Tone has filled pages of his diary with descriptions of their characters and adventures. To the interesting record should be added an account of the life of his own son, William, who seems to have inherited the remarkable family traits of courage, vivacity, and literary and intellectual attainments. The English journalist who recently in the pages of "The Spectator" sneered at Tone as "a poltroon," cannot have been familiar with the history of the family of which he was but one. Courage was inbred in him, as in every one of his kin, and to-day, a hundred years after his death, the Irish race are thanking God that to it was added, in his case, a heroic, unselfish spirit which led him to devote himself to the cause of his suffering country. He stands supreme as one of the most dangerous foes that ever threatened the existence of England's rule in Ireland. Thrice he saw the fleets of friendly nations launched for its destruction; once he brought the army of liberation within near sight of our shores. In Ireland's year of agony and blood, his voice was pleading, with the greatest general since Julius Cæsar for aid for her. If his pleading had been heard, if his advice had been taken earlier in '96 by the Directory, or at any time in '98 by Napoleon, Ireland would have been to-day one of the most important countries in Europe—the outpost of the eastern world—standing between France and America, mid-most of three sister Republics born in that great era of revolution in which the eighteenth century rolled to its end. We would have been celebrating now the Centenary of Independence amid the congratulations of friendly nations and the deferential compliments of fearful or hostile ones. That this is not so is not to be laid to the charge of Wolfe Tone. He did his duty; sacrificed his life for us; and, though victory was not destined for him, we shall not honour, shall not love his memory less. The lowly grave of the Martyr is dearer to us than the proud and pompous tomb of victorious Wellington, who, born in this same city of Dublin, derided the name of Irishman, and chose to serve Ireland's oppressor.

Chapter II.

FROM YOUTH TO MANHOOD.

FROM his earliest childhood, Tone seems to have given promise of remarkable talents. At the first school he attended, without giving steady attention to his duties, he was accustomed to carry off the prizes in all branches of English education at the quarterly examination. It was conducted by the rector of the parish, a Dr. Jamieson, in the presence of the friends and parents of the pupils. This good clergyman joined with the principal of the school, Mr. Darling, in assuring Tone's parents that their boy was too clever to be put to business, and urging them to give him a classical education. They considered that with proper training he would be sure of a fellowship in Trinity College. Tone's father, full of pride and affection, determined to give his boy every chance, and sent him to a good classical school conducted by the Rev. Wm. Craig. Here for a couple of years the boy studied with great diligence at Latin and Greek. As the school was in Stafford Street, he was under his father's eye; but the latter, meeting with an unfortunate accident, found himself after a long illness unable to conduct his business, and decided to move to the County Kildare, where he owned a farm. Rather than disturb the course of Theobald's education, he left him in lodgings with a friend near the school, paying for his residence and giving him a little allowance of pocket money. The boy was scarcely discreet enough to fulfil the trust placed in him, and shortly commenced a system of mitching from school, having calculated that he and his chosen companions could do all the work required of them in three days out of the six. Their leisure time they spent in exploring the country around Dublin; swimming and diving in the blue waters of the bay; and above all, in attending all field days and reviews of the Dublin garrison in Phœnix Park. Anyone who has witnessed one of these splendid pageants on the green sward of the park will understand the fascination such a sight exercised on the heart of a high-spirited, courageous boy. He began to long for a soldier's life, and to regard his destined career at Trinity College with horror. When the time for his entrance drew near, Mr. Craig at last wrote complaining to Tone's father. The result was a violent dispute between father and son. Tone's desire to enter the army was sternly repressed, and he was ordered to recommence his studies. His brother William had run away to join the army from the bookseller's shop where he had been apprenticed; but Theobald was too proud to enlist; he set to work again, and in February, 1781, at the age of eighteen, he entered Trinity. Even after going to College, he renewed his entreaties that he might join the British army, then engaged in America; but the friend of his childhood, the Rev. Dr. Jamieson, and others used their influence successfully in persuading him to yield to his father's wishes, and settle down at college. The idea of the army was then laid aside for ever, and without studying very hard he managed to pass through his college career with some distinction. He took his degree in February, 1786, and shortly afterwards left the college, having to his credit several class premiums, a scholarship, and three medals of the Historical Society, in which he attained the office of auditor. Long before leaving college, he had got over his first antipathy, and had acquired instead a great attachment for old Trinity. But we have not alluded to the most important event of his last college year. More than half a year before taking his degree, without possessing any income on which to support himself, still less a wife—without asking leave of the lady's guardians, or advice of his own parents; without, in fact, consulting anybody but the girl herself, he had gone off and got married. It was a rash step, one that might have wrecked his career of usefulness to Ireland, had he in the blindness of youthful passion fettered himself to an unworthy mate.

Strange to say, this reckless step seems to have been one of the wisest and most salutary actions of his life. Fond of gaiety, and an immense favourite in every company into which he entered, he was exposed to many temptations; but from the time of his marriage he had no higher ideal of happiness than that to be realised at his own fireside. His ardently affectionate disposition, which would have exposed him to many risks, was henceforth safe in the guardianship of one whose devotion and love had nothing in them of ignoble selfishness. The girl-wife, whom Wolfe Tone wooed and won in such a hasty, romantic fashion, turned out to be the best he possibly could have got. His heart's instincts seem to have led him aright in the choice of a wife as in the choice of friends.

It was in the beginning of the year 1785 that they met, or, rather, saw each other first. She was called Matilda Witherington, and was at this time not sixteen years of age. Her grandfather, a wealthy clergyman called Fanning, lived in Grafton Street, Dublin; and as she was uncommonly beautiful, she doubtless attracted the attention of many of the students in the adjoining college. Tone was for some time a silent adorer. Every day after Commons he walked past her window, and though, as he modestly says in his diary, his own appearance was not much in his favour, the attraction was mutual. As yet they had not exchanged a word. In order to gain an introduction and admission to her home, he had recourse to music. She had a brother who played the violin, and with him Tone struck up an acquaintance, being himself something of a musician. Before long he was invited into Mr. Fanning's house, and once so far, he soon became a favourite with everyone; and without much delay he paid court to the lovely girl who had looked down on him from the window with such friendly glances. He found that his love was returned, and asked her promptly to marry him. Without the slightest hesitation, she accepted him; and one beautiful morning in July they ran off together and were married. After spending a few days in Maynooth, in a house which is still pointed out, they returned to Dublin, and took lodgings near the college. The Fanning family forgave their imprudence, and were for a time quite agreeable, and Tone proceeded to study for his degree, deciding after that to read for the Bar.

He was, however, in a somewhat galling and uncomfortable situation—mainly dependent on the family of his wife and without means of support. Soon he was made to feel the ignominy of the position into which he had recklessly plunged. It was impossible for him to longer tolerate the insolence with which his wife's family treated them, so he had no alternative but to leave Dublin for his father's home near Clane, in the County Kildare, and though Peter Tone was then in struggling circumstances, a hearty welcome was extended to the favourite son and his runaway bride.

Chapter III.

ENTERING POLITICS.

THE next period of Tone's life need only be very lightly touched upon. It was probably the least happy. He had not yet found his life-work, nor even his profession or means of livelihood. The marriage which ultimately resulted so fortunately was for a time only a source of embarrassment and anxiety. He had, in fact, to leave his young wife dependent on his father, who was at this time in very poor circumstances, whilst he went to London to pursue his law studies. He was unable to settle down to steady work, and when joined there by his brother William, who had returned from St. Helena, he formulated a scheme of making a settlement in the South Seas; and again, when in more desperate circumstances, he determined to enlist and go abroad. His colonisation scheme was never noticed by the Minister to whom it was submitted, and he was even rejected as a recruit.

On Christmas Day, 1788, he returned to his father's home, after two years' absence, his difficulties being solved by his wife's grandfather paying over her dowry, £500, which had been withheld owing to her runaway marriage. Tone then finished his law studies, and was duly called to the Bar, went the Leinster Circuit some three times and cleared his expenses, but did not care for the life, and clearly saw that he had not yet found his vocation. Hitherto he had been merely an interested spectator of the game of politics. He had grown up in stirring times, had seen the muster of the Volunteers of 1782, and rejoiced at the recognition of the independence of the Irish Parliament. When in London he had contributed articles of a literary and critical nature to the English reviews, and had, in reality, supported himself by his pen and his wits. It was his literary talent which first won him recognition in the political arena. Lord Charlemont, Grattan, and others of the party which had won the Constitution of 1782, had started a body called the Whig Club. It was violently assailed by that portion of the Press which supported the Government. Tone published a pamphlet in their defence, described candidly by himself as being mediocre. However, it was the best thing of the sort that had appeared, and George Ponsonby, on the part of the Whigs, made overtures to the young lawyer, which made him turn his attention to the House of Commons as the goal of his ambitions. He was, moreover, retained as barrister in an election petition case on behalf of the Whigs. Ponsonby seems to have regarded the giving of this brief as attaching Tone to his party; but Tone recognised no obligation either way. He had said a good word for the Whigs; they had employed him in a business transaction. Now that his mind had turned to politics he began to think for himself, and his thoughts, as we know, soon went off the straight and narrow way of Whig traditions. He saw at once straight to the root of all Ireland's ills. It was not English *misgovernment*, but English rule, that was the cause of poverty and discontent. In his new-found faith he was supported by an old friend, Sir Lawrence Parsons (afterwards second Earl of Rosse); in fact, it was Parsons who first turned his attention to the serious consideration of this question. He soon seized an opportunity to express his faith, and when England was apparently on the point of war with Spain, published a pamphlet urging that Ireland was not bound by England's declaration of war. He also advanced without much disguise his ideas on the subject of separation. The pamphlet was suppressed by the printer owing to the denunciation of the first few persons who saw it exposed for sale.

Just about this time he made the acquaintance of a man who was to have an all-important influence on his fate, the dearest, most esteemed of all his friends, Thomas Russell. They met first in the gallery of the Old House of Commons as perfect strangers, and entered into an argument as to the merits of the Whig party. Russell was their staunch admirer; Tone strove, and successfully, to disillusion him. This chance acquaintanceship ripened into close intimacy. Russell became a daily visitor at the seaside cottage at Irishtown, where Tone had brought his young wife for the summer of 1790. Russell's father and Tone's brothers, Matthew and William, were among the other visitors, and in this genial social atmosphere the germs of Tone's democratic opinions ripened apace.

The French Revolution, then in full operation, was turning the minds of thoughtful men to consider stern ways of righting oppression, and all over Ireland the downtrodden people were awakening out of a lethargy.

Tone became notorious for his Republican principles, and ceased to attend the Four Courts, where he knew his opinions would oppose an insuperable barrier to success. In his home circle he found consolation for the absence of worldly prosperity, and his poverty did not prevent his forming friendships with men of learning and distinction.

On returning to Dublin for the winter of 1790, he became the presiding genius of a literary and political *coterie* which included John Stack, F.T.C.D.; Wm. Drennan, Peter Burrowes, Wm. Johnson, Thos. Addis Emmet, and Whitley Stokes. Tone's club did not turn out such a success as he had anticipated. "This experiment," he writes, "satisfied me that men of genius do not work well in the aggregate. . . . The dullest entertainment at which I ever remember to have assisted was one formed expressly to bring together near twenty persons, every one more or less distinguished for splendid talents or great convivial qualities. . . . Any two of the men present would have been the delight and entertainment of a well-chosen society, but all together was, as Wolsey says, '*too much honour.*'"

In the list of members of this club you will notice the name of Thomas Emmet, destined to become prominent in connection with Tone's later career; you will have remarked also the absence of the name of the friend whose geniality had brightened the gatherings at the summer cottage in Irishtown. Thomas Russell, who was in the army, had been ordered to join a regiment in Belfast, and whilst Tone was engaged with this unsuccessful experiment the young officer had become one of the most popular figures in political circles in the North, and with all the ardour of a recent convert was spreading the faith which Tone had inculcated. *The English connection, not England's misgovernment, is Ireland's bane.* This doctrine found ready acceptance among the sturdy dissenters of the Northern town. Many of the leading spirits were in fact already Republicans, and in sympathy with the French Revolutionists. But to understand the important part which the people of Belfast played in that eventful era, we must look back a few years in history.

Chapter IV.

THE UNITED IRISH CLUBS FOUNDED.

AS long ago as 1783 the Belfast Volunteer delegates to the Dublin Convention had advocated complete Catholic emancipation. Their liberal views did not meet with general support amongst the Protestant patriots; but their bold demand for religious freedom alarmed the Government to such an extent that they procured from Lord Kenmare a disavowal of the claim. This base subserviency stung the Catholic Committee into action, and, assembling in a Convention, they repudiated Lord Kenmare, and reiterated the claims of the Belfast Volunteers. This had taken place in the year 1783, and Thomas Russell on arriving in Belfast apparently made an effort to persuade the Volunteers to make a similar declaration. He wrote to his friend Tone to draw up the declaration, and it was in due time put before a meeting of the corps. It became, however, apparent that there would be some strong opposition offered to it, and the promoters seeing the time not ripe wisely withdrew it. Russell wrote to Tone a full account of the proceedings. The unexpected opposition stirred the latter to serious meditation on the causes of disunion and servitude, and in due course he wrote and published a powerful pamphlet addressed to the Dissenters of Ireland under the title, "An Argument on Behalf of the Catholics of Ireland."

It is in his own account of the origin of this pamphlet that Tone embodies his famous confession of faith.

> To subvert the tyranny of our execrable Government, to break the connection with England, the never-failing source of all our political

evils, and to assert the independence of my country, these were my objects. To unite the whole people of Ireland, to abolish the memory of all past dissensions, and to substitute the common name of Irishmen in place of the denominations of Protestant, Catholic, Dissenter, these were my means.

He despaired of converting the Episcopalian party, and took the anti-English feeling of the Irish Catholics for granted. His appeal was, therefore, addressed to the dissenters, its object, as he states it—

To convince them that they and the Catholics had but one common interest and one common enemy; that the depression and slavery of Ireland was produced and perpetuated by the divisions existing between them, and that consequently to assert the independence of their country, and their own individual liberties, it was necessary to forget all former feuds, to consolidate the entire strength of the whole nation, and to form for the future one people.

This pamphlet appeared in September, 1791 (when Tone was 28), over the signature of "A Northern Whig." It had a large circulation, being distributed broadcast by the Catholics and dissenters, and it brought the author (till then a stranger) into immediate contact with both parties. John Keogh, who had now taken the lead in the Catholic Committee, introduced him to all the important members; and in the next year, 1792, he succeeded Richard Burke as paid secretary; but before he became connected with the Catholic organisation he was already a member, and, indeed, founder of a new body specially formed as a practical experiment to embody the principles of Union advocated in his pamphlet. In October, 1791, Russell, who had left the army, came to Dublin, and asked Tone to accompany him to Belfast. He had been elected an honorary member of the Green Company of Belfast Volunteers, and the Northern democrats were eager to make the acquaintance of their new comrade.

A full account of that memorable visit is recorded in Tone's diary. We can only briefly sum up the result of it, which was his establishing, in conjunction with Russell, Neilson, and others, the first club of

UNITED IRISHMEN.

Samuel Neilson, Thomas M'Cabe, the brothers Simms, William Sinclair, Henry Joy and William M'Cracken were amongst the most prominent members.

On returning to Dublin Tone approached Napper Tandy, the most popular Protestant on the patriot side, and put him in touch with some of the Catholic party. A United Club was then formed, which adopted the constitution of the Belfast body (drawn up by Tone), and entered into correspondence with it. Strange to say, Tone retained little influence in the councils of this Dublin Club, and except for a short period, when he acted as *locum tenens* for Napper Tandy in the secretaryship, he had no office in it.

It was left to the Catholics of Dublin to recognise and make use of the talents of the young patriot, and in the year 1792 he was appointed assistant secretary to the Catholic Committee with a salary of £200 a year. The Society had adopted, on the suggestion of Myles Keon (a Leitrim man), a new constitution, according to which they summoned representatives from towns and counties on the Parliamentary system, to confer on all important occasions. For the first time the Committee was really entitled to act on behalf of the Catholics of all Ireland. In organising for the Catholic Convention, Tone visited Connaught, and in July 1792, he revisited Belfast, to be present at a great Volunteer review, held on the anniversary of the fall of the Bastille. The occasion of this popular demonstration is self-evident proof of the fact that Republicanism was by this time rampant in the Northern town.

In a great assembly, held after the review in the Linen Hall Square, a congratulatory address was voted unanimously to the French people. It was followed by an address being voted to the people of Ireland, in which the Catholic claims were boldly asserted. Tone's pamphlet had taken effect. The opposition which Russell had met with previous to its publication had sunk to a mere whisper, and as he stood there under the shadow of the Linen Hall, and heard the unanimous acclaim which hailed the demand for religious equality, Tone might have proudly taken to himself the glory of having wakened the voice of a United Ireland. In December of the same year he was present at the great Catholic Convention, the first representative gathering of Irish Catholics held since the reign of James II. On that occasion he was entitled to claim the credit of organising the country and helping to inspire the assembly with a bold and determined spirit.

In the spring of 1793 the agitation in which the Catholic Committee had been engaged resulted in the Government passing a partial measure of relief, which became law on April 9th. Tone has summed up the advantages granted by the Bill as follows:—

By one comprehensive clause all penalties, forfeitures, disabilities and incapacities are removed; the property of the Catholic is completely discharged from the restraints and limitations of the penal laws, and their liberty in a great measure restored by the restoration of the right of elective franchise, so long withheld and so ardently pursued. The right of self-defence is established by the restoration of the privilege to carry arms, subject to a restraint, which does not seem unreasonable as excluding none but the very lowest orders. The unjust and unreasonable distinctions affecting Catholics as to service on grand and petty juries are done away; the army, navy, and all offices and places of trust are opened to them subject to exceptions hereafter mentioned.

He then points out that, in spite of the relief granted, the penal system was maintained by clauses in the Bill excluding Catholics from sitting in Parliament or filling the higher offices of state—

By granting the Franchise and withholding seats in Parliament, the Catholic gentry are at once compelled and enabled to act with effect as a distinct body and separate interest. They receive a benefit with one hand and a blow with the other, and their rising gratitude is checked by just resentment. . . As the law now stands a Catholic gentleman of the first rank and fortune is in a political point of view inferior to the meanest of his tenants; combining their situation and their feelings, *they* are fully emancipated, *he* drags along an unseemly and galling link of his ancient chain.

In the same session of Parliament which saw this measure of relief become law, two coercive measures were passed —one, "*The Convention Act*," made illegal such assemblies as that Catholic Convention which had forced this partial emancipation from the Government; the other, "*The Gunpowder Act*," forbade the importation of arms and ammunition, and gave to the magistrates that power of search which was so terribly misused in the following years. Thus were the Catholics given a sop to pacify them, and deprived at the same time of the means of remonstrance or revolt. Tone was anxious to pursue the agitation further, and urged that they should not rest satisfied with less than complete emancipation.

Chapter V.

CONCILIATION AND CONSPIRACY.

AT the end of the year 1794, Lord Fitzwilliam replaced Lord Westmoreland as Viceroy, and in February, '95, Grattan, with Fitzwilliam's approbation, brought in a Bill for the admission of Catholics into Parliament. The machinations of the anti-Catholic party, directed by Fitzgibbon (Lord Clare) resulted in the recall of Fitz-

william and the destruction of the people's hopes of this final emancipation. It is argued by some historians and many platform speakers that it was the disappointment caused by Fitzwilliam's recall which turned the thoughts of the people towards revolution; but certain events were transpiring during that very year of hope which prove conclusively that that the United Irishmen were known outside of Ireland to be Republicans in principle and aiming at the liberation of Ireland.

To those who point to the British Government as the cause of the United Conspiracy, we would say, remember the Belfast Demonstration celebrating the fall of the Bastile in 1792, and that when Tone, in November, 1791, asked Napper Tandy to initiate the first club of Dublin United Irishmen he did so because that famous personage was, to quote his (Tone's) words, "a very sincere Republican, who did not require much argument to show him the impossibility of attaining a Republic by any means short of the united powers of the whole people." Recollect, too, that at the very outset Tone reckoned on finding in every Catholic Irishman the making of a rebel, and addressed his famous pamphlet to the Dissenters who stood in need of conversion, whereas of the Catholics he says:—

"I well knew that, however it might be disguised or suppressed, there existed in the breast of every Irish Catholic an inextirpable abhorrence of English name and power."

To return to the era of Fitzwilliam's Viceroyalty. Before he had even set foot in the country, Irish Republicanism had found recognition in France, and an envoy sent by the Committee of Public Safety had made the acquaintance of Theobald Wolfe Tone, and had secured from him a written declaration on the state of Ireland, which was tantamount to an appeal for French aid. This envoy was the Rev. Wm. Jackson, an Anglican clergyman of Irish descent and democratic sympathies.

Jackson was unfortunately in the hands of informers from the outset, and his first interview with Tone took place in the presence of the notorious Leonard M'Nally. He suggested that Tone should go to France to represent the state of Ireland, and in view of later events it is interesting to notice that the latter regarded it beyond the bounds of possibility that he could undertake such a mission, and states as his reason—

"I was a man of no fortune; my sole dependence was in a profession; I had a wife and three children, whom I dearly loved, solely dependent on me for support, and could not go and leave them totally unprovided for and trusting to the mercy of Providence for existence."

In April, '94, Jackson was arrested, Pitt having been informed of his mission from the outset. Hamilton Rowan, who had been in communication with him was in prison, but made good his escape and reached France; Dr. Reynolds also left the country; but Tone resolved to brave the matter out. His sudden flight would have been a fatal blow to the National movement, as his influence and connection extended now to every part of the country. As secretary of the Catholic Committee he had his associates to think of, and if he had fled his self-acknowledged treason would have tainted the whole body. He took a very daring and still prudent step by going to a member of the Government and making a plain statement which involved only himself. He did so on condition that he would not be called in Jackson's trial, and absolutely refused, even at a private inquiry, to make any statement on oath. Jackson was kept a twelve-month in prison, and in the month following his arrest the Government dispersed the United Irishmen's meeting in Back Lane, and forbade their re-assembling. The more timid members deserted; but those who owned to staunch Republican principles adhered to the Society, which, in the year 1795, became secret, oath-bound, and infinitely more dangerous and resolute.

At length, after Fitzwilliam had left the country, and Camden's rule of iron had been substituted, Jackson was brought up for trial. Tone's friends in power kept faith with him, and he was not called as a witness. Witnesses, in fact, were not necessary, as Pitt knew all through his spies. One of them, Cockayne, appeared in the witness-box, the other, Leonard M'Nally, hid his treachery, and remained in the confidence of the Unitedmen. Curran appeared for Jackson, who was nevertheless found guilty, and brought up for sentence. He took poison, and died tragically in the dock. Ten days later the secret constitution and oath of the United Irishmen was framed. Tone, the founder of the Society, was at the time under sentence of banishment to America, and busied with his preparations for departure. He confided to two trusted friends, Russell and Thomas Emmet, the full story of his compromise with the Government, and rejoiced with them that he was under no bond and had undertaken no obligation in return for his freedom. The conversation took place as he walked in from Emmet's villa at Rathfarnham. He told them that he considered his exile as a full expiation for the offence, and felt at liberty to begin again on a fresh score; that in Philadelphia he intended to find out the French Minister, and obtain introductions to Paris. In fact Jackson's plan, which he had scouted as impossible, was about to be realised; the dead envoy of France to Ireland was to be replaced by Ireland's envoy to France, and Wolfe Tone was to fill that position.

Chapter VI.

GOOD-BYE TO DUBLIN.

IN the month of May, 1795, Wolfe Tone spent his last days of happiness and freedom in his native city. There is no better proof of his attractiveness and personal worth given us than his own account of the attitude of his friends and acquaintances towards him during that time when he lay under suspicion. His behaviour was characteristically courageous and defiant. He scorned to remain in seclusion, and on the very day of Jackson's trial was to be seen sauntering up and down the principal streets of Dublin. Carrying his *sang froid* a step further, he strolled into several of the most frequented coffee houses, places where, as in the clubs of our own day, current politics were discussed, and where, he informs us, he was not a usual visitor. We can imagine the scene. The conspiracy trial is the subject of excited argument amongst the groups of politicians—lawyers, merchants, students—who are sipping coffee over their newspapers. The name of Tone is mentioned here, there, and everywhere as being deeply implicated. Some of the sage Whig M.P.'s shake their heads gravely and say they all along had an idea that he was an unsafe character to deal with. He had tried to push his way into their party, but had been put off by those who knew better than to encourage him. In connection with the Catholic agitation he had always been a reckless, hotheaded fellow, not safe to have dealings with, not at all safe. They were well rid of him. He would now have to clear out of the country, if he had not already made good his escape. Then a kind word was put in for him by someone who had been a fellow-student and fallen under the spell of his attractive personality. Jonah Barrington, if

he was about, spoke up for him. He had taken quite an interest in the young fellow, and tried to give him a helping hand to keep him out of mischief, going so far as to share his coach with him when he went on circuit, for he was very hard up, had made a devilish imprudent marriage, and could scarcely afford the expenses of his profession. Then, when his name was thus on everyone's lips, in walked Tone, cool as a cucumber, nodded pleasantly to several acquaintances, but did not stay long or obtrude his compromising society upon any of them. A glance at the news of the day and a few remarks about the weather or the new play, and on he went to startle the gossipers at some other coffee house in the same fashion. Lastly, he went to what was the most frequented place of all, his bookseller's, and here he was stared at by no less a person than Lord Mountjoy, who rushed off to inform the Attorney-General that Mr. Tone, if wanted, was still in town. The Attorney-General of the time was Wolfe, afterwards Lord Kilwarden. He gave Mountjoy little thanks for his pains, being, of course, aware of Tone's arrangement to leave Ireland on condition that he should not be called on in Jackson's trial. This was not the last service he did for him; we may assume that he was one of those who, like Barrington, had taken a liking for him. As we shall see, it was this same Kilwarden who stood between the patriot and the hangman's rope at a time when he lay dying from his self-inflicted wound, and when the brutal Court-martial would have dragged him, all the same, to the scaffold and the noose. Tone adds in his account of Mountjoy's eagerness to have him prosecuted a remark to the effect that he " gave his Lordship credit for his intentions." How he would have relished that part of the Wexford ballad which says.—

        A young man from our ranks,
        A cannon he let go,
        And slapped it into Lord Mountjoy—
        A tyrant he laid low.

That young man from the Wexford ranks paid off Wolfe Tone's score against the tyrant anyhow. Having walked around to show himself, Tone commenced to dispose of his household effects. All his little property was sold off except his library of six hundred volumes. Like a good book-lover, he reserved these to brighten his life in the Far West, where books were not so easily to be picked up as on the Dublin quays. He made up his mind not to compromise anyone by paying a single farewell visit. He was prepared for coldness and even for desertion, and as he busied himself packing and sorting his books and going to and from the salerooms where his household treasures were being sent for disposal, he steeled his heart to endure with fortitude the worst coldness and unkindness that faithless human nature could show towards him in misfortune. But just in this dark hour the worth of his friends was proved. As soon as the news got abroad that he was about to leave Ireland, they came pouring in to show their sympathy, give their help, and in most cases to discuss the outlook of "*the Cause.*" Even those who thought differently in politics came to see the last of him. The house was rarely an hour without a visitor, and the brave-hearted young wife had not time to sit down and mope or brood over the future.

M'Cormick and Keogh, the Catholic leaders, were among the first to call, and the news they brought was welcome. They had been mainly representative in getting the Catholic Committee to deal generously with the late energetic Secretary. All arrears of salary due to him were promptly paid up, with an additional parting gift of £300. With these two trusted colleagues Tone discussed the scheme which had been approved of by his more intimate personal friends, Emmet and Russell, that spring day as they walked from Rathfarnham into town. Keogh and M'Cormick gave their most cordial approbation; urged him without fail to make his way to France and ask for armed assistance. They assured him that, if he succeeded, there was no honour Ireland could bestow but he could fairly claim. They most likely intended thus to promise him their influence with the Catholic party in making him President of the Irish Republic. Their promise was not rashly nor unadvisedly given. They had experience of Tone's capacity, energy, and enthusiasm, his power of organising. They were aware that these qualities had gained for him a following of devoted adherents in every part of the country, and that if he crowned his services to Ireland by bringing to her shores a French invasion to co-operate in liberating her, he would be the idol of the grateful people, and that the glory of being first President of the Republic would be assuredly his.

At times, we can see by Tone's diary, the same dazzling prospect seemed possible to him, and yet, since ambition was not his ruling passion, he did not let it delude or allure him. From first to last he was facing danger and difficulty, inspired purely by a sense that it was his duty to do a man's part to right Ireland's intolerable wrongs. In those last days, however, the affection and confidence shown him by his friends must have deeply touched him. He felt that great things were expected of him, and the resolve to justify such expectation was strengthened and confirmed.

In regard to the promise he had given to leave the country, he felt that all obligation on his side ended when he went into exile. The Irish Government had exacted no *parole* from him in regard to his nor meddling in politics, and had made no objection to his going to Philadelphia, where they were well aware there was a French Minister resident. They probably did not consider Tone a seriously dangerous person, or were too assured of Britain's security from

French attack. As subsequent events proved, they would have done better to have exiled him to India, which Tone says was the first place proposed.

It was mid-May when at length, with his wife, his sister Maria, and his three little children, he drove away northward from Dublin. The parting with his father and mother was painful, for they were an exceedingly affectionate family, and, though every one of the Tones was by nature an adventurer and wanderer, home love seemed to be with each a ruling passion. Strange contradiction, but true! The scene of his boyhood, of his gay college days, of his love, of his happy married life, was now left behind for ever— but he had not left Ireland yet. There were other friends of Freedom to be consulted; other farewells to take. Belfast was to be the port of embarkation, and thither along the Northern coach road the band of wanderers now made their way.

Chapter VII.

LAST DAYS IN IRELAND.

"*Oh, I'll go down into Belfast and see that seaport gay.*"

N Belfast a regular ovation awaited him. The politicians of this lively town had been among the first to do him public honour, and as they were the leaders of Protestant Nationalism, it was important that he should have their approval of his "foreign policy," and be authorised to speak on their behalf, as Keogh and M'Cormick had authorised him to speak for the Catholic Nationalists of Ireland. For nearly a month Tone remained in Belfast feted and entertained daily, not only by his friends, but by many who

were scarcely acquainted with him, but were eager for the pleasure. The taint of treason to the British Crown had done him no harm in the eyes of the Ulster Republicans. One day the tent of the first regiment of the Volunteers was pitched in the Deer Park, and the families of the Simms, Neilsons, and M'Cracken camped out from morning till evening. The Neilson children played with little Mary and William. Mary M'Cracken and her sisters were there, Mary possibly taking more interest in the talk of the men than in the children's sports or the preparations for dinner, and regarding with greatest admiration handsome, dark-eyed Thomas Russell, who, if he had by this time recovered from his infatuation for lovely Bess Goddard, was paying his devoirs to Miss Simms, the sister of Robert and William.

When Mr. Russell was hiding among the Belfast hills with a price upon his head a few years later, Mary M'Cracken was the first of his friends who had courage to visit him. Through her he sent a message to arrange an interview with his lady-love, but, alas! that lady was faithless, or cold, or cowardly. It is often asserted, without grounds, that Russell was engaged to Miss M'Cracken. The fact is that within a few weeks of his death he thus made her the medium of communication with another woman. After the latter showed herself so heartless, Mary M'Cracken's devoted friendship must have awakened the deepest and most affectionate regard, but love-making or betrothal were out of the question.

I am scarcely digressing in alluding to the events of the year 1803, as I wish the reader to realise the relationships of friendship or romance which existed amongst those social gatherings in Belfast a hundred years ago. It may have been on this pic-nic occasion that little Mary Tone, who had a fresh, pretty voice, was called on to sing for the assembled company a song to the air of the *Cruiscín Lán* which her father had taught her and written words for.

Music was a feature at every one of the parties, for Mr. Edward Bunting, the organist of St. Anne's, had caused quite a musical revival in Belfast. Tone was exceedingly musical, and we shall see him later on jotting down about fifty airs suitable for Irish regimental band-playing. At one of these gatherings the pathos of a song played by Mr. Bunting, *The Parting of Friends*, proved too much for the wife of Tone. Her pent-up emotions gave way, and, dissolved in tears, she rushed from the room. The gloom of the coming cloud of sorrow made its presence felt among the erstwhile gay company.

Alas! in a few short years prison and death and exile were to sever the friends who sat there listening to the heart-touching music. It was not at the social supper or over the wine cups that his future plan of action was discussed and agreed to. The junketing of the monster demonstration days was over. Resolutions passed at Volunteer parades amid the waving of green and tri-colour banners to the sound of bands and the cheering of multitudes had now to be translated into the more quiet and dangerous form of a secret, steadfast resolve taken under solemn and binding auspices by a few men who trusted each other, and were willing to stand by their resolve to the death.

The place chosen for this council was a fitting and sublime one. Let us picture it ere we proceed, for in truth it is one of the most sacred spots within the four seas of Erin.

Northward from Belfast, facing the Scottish shore, there is a hill which, outlined against the heavens, resembles the profile face of some sleeping giant. Not a grim and rugged face this, but of perfect beauty and proportion. The brow, the lips, the curving throat, the firmly-chiselled, slightly-indented chin, later on reminded the Belfast United Men returned from Paris of the great world-conquering Napoleon, who they thought might yet be Ireland's deliverer. To this day the people of Belfast, even those who hate France and uphold England's rule, call it "Napoleon's Face." They do the exile of Helena high honour by thus naming the mountain monument upon Ireland's shore. England was his enemy, his gaoler; therefore, we would hardly care to abolish this popular nomenclature; and yet—and yet linked with the memory of Napoleon our Cave Hill is but the monument of disappointed hopes, a reminder of the flotillas that he sent to Egypt at the very season when the peasants of Ireland, in death grapples with the tyrant, might have been saved by armaments of France; a reminder, too, of the empty promises that dazzled young Robert Emmet and lured him to his desperate enterprise and early doom. This sacred hill, so strangely beautiful in its statuesque grandeur, suggests to the imaginative soul a vaguer and more touching ideal. It is the image of Freedom that slumbers there—Sovereign Freedom, the same goddess whose image the grandsons of those French Republicans sent in these latter days as a gift of friendship to America. On the shores of that Western world she lifts her enlightening torch to guide the incoming ships of many nations. Irishmen, whom this year of memories brings from America's shore, when the torch of liberty flares upon your sight, look not upon it enviously. In Ireland you will see a vaster, fairer image of Freedom. God, not man, was her sculptor; the glaciers and fires moulded her. She has been here since the beginning of the world—since before the creation of that human race in whose likeness God made her.

Two days were passed by Tone and a party of his patriot friends in roaming over the rocks, heath, and brushwood of Cave Hill. It is a pleasant place to ramble in, and we may be sure that in those two days the whole hill was thoroughly explored. Russell, who was something of a botanist, and who had been for years resident in Belfast, by this time knew every nook of it—the rock-encircled cavities below the cliffs, which Samuel Ferguson describes in his historical tales; the natural cairns and tussocks, the stretches of mossy sward, the woods at the base, with the brooklet trinkling through. It was June or latter May, and the gorse was still in flaming bloom along the heights. The bluebells made a misty blue; the white thorns snowed down their petals. Somewhere in a pleasant spot, most likely near the brook, they pic-niced, but it was on the topmost crest of the hill that at length they reclined for that talk which has become historic.

Chapter VIII.

THE VOW ON M'ART'S FORT.

THE highest point of the Cave Hill is an immense crag, which descends to the seaward side in several hundred feet of sheer precipice. Here in olden times some warlike tribe of the Gael had on the other side entrenched it, making it into a strongly-fortified place. It cannot have been used for habitation, but a group of dwellings with a chieftain's dun likely stood lower on the hill. This was their post of outlook — the place where the beacon fire was kindled to gather the clan in time of war. Here, likely, such hill councils were held as Spenser has described. Here the chieftain was inaugurated, taking his oath at the stones that are piled throne-like upon the verge of the precipice. These stones are mainly natural rocks, but till lately on their summit was poised a boulder that must have been brought there. In it was a cavity that fitted the right hand like a gauntlet. Sir Samuel Ferguson suggested that in the inaugural ceremony on Cave Hill the chieftain may have taken his oath with his *hand* in the stone, thus varying the usual custom of standing with the foot on a track shaped like a footprint.

This may have been so, but no antiquarian can now view this famous stone or theorise on its use; some ignorant, reckless person within the past year amused himself by hurling it over the verge of the precipice, and seeing it crash to fragments on the crags below.

Around this inaugural throne of warlike chieftains on that day of summer, 1795, the group of patriot friends assembled to take serious council as to what should be done and dared for Ireland's cause. There was Thomas Russell, handsome, stately in demeanour, checking with an occasional utterance, in his musical Southern voice, any approach to flippancy on the part of the others, and with that serious demeanour which made Tone give him the *soubriquet,* " *Priest of the Parish,*" impressing on everyone that this was a solemn occasion. There was Sam Neilson, the outspoken journalist, editor of the "Northern Star" newspaper. There was one of the Simms brothers, most likely Robert, the man who was chosen to lead Ulster in '98, and who through over-caution failed to do his duty at the appointed hour. There was Henry Joy M'Cracken, who was to dash into that dilatory general's place, and order the army of Ulster forward against Antrim town. There were one or two others not mentioned by Tone—Thomas M'Cabe, perhaps, father of the famous Putnam M'Cabe, himself a patriot, and John Tennant, who went to prison with Neilson, Russell, and the rest within two years, and whom we shall meet later on in Paris accompanying Tone to an interview with General Bonaparte. There they sat reclined on the green sward whilst Wolfe Tone unfolded his thoughts as to the possibility of gaining Ireland's independence, arguing that nothing less than an Irish Republic should satisfy patriot Irishmen, and that it was their duty to stake their lives for the winning of it. He for one meant to do so. Though he must cross the ocean and leave Ireland, he was not forsaking Ireland's cause. Across half the world he would carry hate of England in his heart, and maybe find outside of Ireland means of subverting her tyrant sway. Stirred to the hearts by this declaration, his comrades one by one reached their hands to him and repeated that solemn pledge to devote their lives to the achievement of Ireland's freedom.

Then they rose, descended from the hilltop by the winding path among the rocks, or else along the heathy slope nearest the town. The old fort of the Son of Art had from that moment and will have till the end of time an added glory and dignity. In the eyes of all patriots it is sacred ground, to be looked on reverently as an altar. The God in whose presence that vow was taken had destined three of those who uttered it to yield up their lives in expiation.

Just within two days of his departure Tone spent at Ram's Island, in Lough Neagh, what he describes as the happiest day of all, and one of the most agreeable in his life. It speaks volumes for the pure and simple character of the man that what contributed to make one day so joyous, so memorable, that he promised to commemorate its anniversary till the end of his life was no more than this:—A bright day of perfect summer, a boat upon the blue waters of an Irish lake, a pic-nic under the bushes in a green island, with the scent of flowers and the freshness of the breeze from the lake; about him his children playing among the bushes or at the waters edge; their mother, the woman he loved best in the world, by his side, innocently happy as himself; his sister there, and his best and truest friend and comrade.

Happier far and more elate than when as a schoolboy he roamed the glades of Phœnix Park, yet with all a boy's unrestrained glee, he helped at the pic-nic meal, or maybe insisted on P.P. acting as cook, as on that day long ago when in all the glory of his gold-laced regimentals he was delegated to the kitchen of the Sandymount cottage. There were jests and laughter and song—laughter to chase away the sad thoughts, jests to quell the tears that arose in the eyes of wife and sister if ever silence came. And, realising the scene, our own tears are like to rise when we remember that this happy day was the last in life that ever those true friends spent together. Only three anniversaries of it were to be celebrated by Tone; a few more were to pass over and Russell was to be standing on the scaffold at Downpatrick. Through long widowed years, bereft of all save one child, the patriot's wife was to live on, the sole celebrant of that happy day.

On the 13th June Tone and his family embarked at Belfast Quay on board the Cincinnatus of Wilmington. From his brief account we can gather that he had a great send-off. The kind Belfast friends vied with each other in contributing to the comfort of the emigrants. A cabin with three berths was secured for their sole use, and in it stores of food and sweetmeats were packed. Dr. M'Donnell, the constant friend of Russell, contributed a regular medicine chest, and wrote out directions for the use of the various bottles and powders in case of sea-sickness and other ailments. He, in fact, qualified Tone to act as ship doctor, which post we shall see he actually assumed. Not only did his personal friends flock around him, but he tells us that some who had been cold and estranged returned to show him civility and kindness. There was an addition to the emigrant party which gave him great pleasure. This was his youngest brother, Arthur, a boy of fourteen, whom he describes in his diary as the vagrant of the family. He had taken this lad's part when Peter Tone, the father, wanted to apprentice him to an attorney, and had saved him from being fettered to a career for which he was entirely unfitted. At his suggestion the boy had been allowed to make one voyage, and at twelve years of age had sailed to Portugal. Returning more than ever fond of the sea, he was regularly apprenticed, and, landing from a voyage at the port of Belfast in June, '95, he found his eldest brother just about to sail for America. The brothers were mutually rejoiced. Wolfe Tone saw that Arthur would be useful, as he could be sent back to Ireland with a message, so he persuaded him to come on board the Cincinnatus, likely arranging for him to work his passage out.

So on June 13th, the wind being favourable, the ship went down from the harbour out past Carrickfergus Roads. The blue ridge of Cave Hill vanished as they rounded Islandmagee and sailed westward from Belfast Lough.

Of the friends whom they left on the quay, three had been entrusted with Tone's design of leaving America for France. These were Simms, Sam Neilson, and C. H. Teeling —the latter a young Catholic gentleman belonging to Lisburn, who had great influence among the clubs of the Defenders, secret societies formed by the oppressed Catholics of Ulster to withstand persecution. The Ancient Order of Hibernians of America is the successor of this organisation, and will rightly take its place in the Centenary celebrations. In Ireland the necessity for Defenderism has long since passed away, and we would wish to see those who perpetuate organisations formed on lines which promote party strife lay them aside and take their place in the ranks of the men who are striving to promote, as Wolfe Tone did, Union amongst all Nationalist Irishmen.

Chapter IX.

TONE IN AMERICA.

THE voyage to America was a very different thing in those days from what it is at present, and even now we hear complaints of the hardship which the steerage passengers have to endure in their comparatively short journey occupying a week or ten days. It was upwards of eight weeks before Tone reached the American shore, and during all that time he was an inmate of an overcrowded emigrant ship. With his wife, three children, and sister he occupied one cabin of small dimensions; but in his diary there is scarcely a word of grumbling about the discomforts they must have suffered. His indignation is reserved for the treatment meted out to the poor emigrants, of whom there were three hundred on board. He did all in his power to alleviate their lot, which he describes as follows:—

"The slaves who are carried from the coast of Africa have much more room allowed them than the miserable emigrants who pass from Ireland to America, for the avarice of the captains in that trade is such that they think they never can load their vessels sufficiently, and they trouble their heads in general no more about the accommodation and storage of their passengers than of any other lumber aboard. I laboured, and with some degree of success, to introduce something like a police and a certain degree, though a very imperfect one, of cleanliness among them. Certainly the air of the sea must be wonderfully wholesome, for if the same number of wretches of us had been shut up in the same space ashore, with so much inconvenience of every kind about us, two-thirds of us would have died in the time of our voyage. As it was, in spite of everything, we were tolerably healthy; we lost but one passenger, a woman. We had some sick aboard, and the friendship of James M'Donnell, of Belfast, having supplied me with a small medicine chest and written directions, I took on myself the office of physician. I prescribed and administered accordingly, and I had the satisfaction to land all my patients safe and sound. As we distributed liberally the surplus of our sea-stores, of which we had a great abundance, and especially as we gave from time to time wine and porter to the sick and aged, we soon became very popular aboard, and I am sure there was no sacrifice to our ease or convenience in the power of our poor fellow passengers to make that we might not have commanded."

No wonder Wolfe Tone commands the love of the exiles of our race. Is there a more beautiful picture than this of the patriot, bending over the sick and aged with words of gentleness and comfort, finding out their ailments, and bringing them remedies and nourishment? Think of him going into the unclean, crowded dens and trying to restore order and cleanliness among the poor people, who were herded together like cattle!

A stirring event disturbed the monotony of the voyage. It was one which deepened, if possible, his hate towards Britain. Three British frigates swooped down upon the Cincinnatus ere she reached the kindly shelter of America's shore, whilst they were passing the banks of Newfoundland. Fifty of the emigrants were carried off by the press-gang to help to man the navy. Tone narrowly escaped the same fate, having been actually seized by the lieutenant in command, he being dressed in a seamanlike costume. The entreaties of his wife and sister saved him, and he stood to watch in fierce indignation the kidnapping of the poor emigrants. "The insolence of these tyrants as well to myself," he writes, "as to my poor fellow-passengers, in whose fate a fellowship in misfortune had interested me, I have never forgotten, and I never will." Perhaps there were some of these kidnapped emigrants among the seamen whose mutiny at the Nore crippled the British fleet a short time later.

Wolfe Tone's stay in America was not destined to extend over a longer period than five months. He was here only as a bird of passage, France being his real goal. The first place he inhabited on American soil was the chief tavern or hotel in Wilmington, which was kept by an Irishman rejoicing in the name of Captain O'Byrne O'Flynn. He corroborates the well-known joke as to the population of America being "mostly colonels," telling us that "all the taverns in America are kept by majors and captains either of militia or continentals." Of course, this prevalence of military titles was a result of the recent War of Independence. The first new friend with whom the Tones took up was a General Humpton, who had fought through it on the American side, though he was an Englishman born in Yorkshire. This veteran showed the emigrant family every kindness and attention, and found them a lodging in Philadelphia, to which they removed a week after landing.

Here he met with Dr. Reynolds, an old friend, who informed him that no less a person than Archibald Hamilton Rowan had landed some weeks before from France. That very evening the three exiles met and recounted their several adventures. Rowan had been well received in France. After suffering some temporary inconvenience by imprisonment as an English spy, he had been maintained by the French Government; but during the confusion consequent on the fall of Robespierre he saw no prospect of serving Ireland, and, therefore, emigrated to the States.

This meeting with Hamilton Rowan seemed providentially opportune to Tone, as he saw the recommendations of a person who had already formed a connection in France would be advantageous to himself. Immediately he confided his own designs to Rowan, who offered to conduct him to the French Minister, Citizen Adet, whom he had known in Paris. Tone, apprehending that British spies would be on the alert to notice his movements, said it would be less noticeable if he went alone to visit the Minister, merely bringing a letter of introduction from Rowan.

This was agreed to, and accordingly next day he presented himself at the office of the Minister, and was accorded a most polite reception; but, alas! he found himself at a loss to make himself understood. Adet knew little English, Tone less French. The conversation was not very satisfactory to either, and after scanning Tone's recommendations from Ireland and Rowan's letter, Adet suggested that anything he had to communicate should be drawn up in the form of a written memorial. For the next two or three days Tone worked hard at this stiff job, greatly impeded by his imperfect knowledge of French and discomforted by the intense summer heat, to which he was yet entirely unaccustomed. Literally, as well as metaphorically, we may say that Tone on coming to America "took off his coat." After much difficulty the memorial was ready, and Tone stated that he was prepared to start to France by the first ship. The Minister's breath was taken away by this hasty manner of doing business, and he threw difficulties in the way. He promised, however, to do all in his power to secure the release of Matthew Tone, who was in prison in Guise on suspicion of being a spy.

Tone seemed depressed by the cold reception given to his memorial, and commenced to make arrangements for settling down in America in case that this should, after all, be his destiny. He moved his family from Philadelphia, where the cost of living was immense, and resided first in Westchester, then in Downingstown, in the State of Pennsylvania. Leaving them to the care of General Humpton, he started out in search of a farm to purchase, journeying sometimes on foot, sometimes on stage waggons. Near Princeton, in New Jersey, he at length found a suitable farm for sale, for which he commenced negotiations. Then, hiring a house for the winter, he brought his family there, unpacked his books, and, fitting up his study, was quite ready to settle down, with no other prospect for the present than that of becoming an American farmer. However, fortunately, the title deeds were not yet signed when letters arrived from Ireland which roused him to action. These were from John Keogh, the Catholic leader; from Russell, and William Simms, and all three urged him to lose no time in making his way to France. Simms added an offer of £200 to cover expenses.

These letters gave him a pretext to renew his application to Adet, but, first of all, he placed them before his wife and sister, whose comfort and welfare he was bound to consider, and he never doubted but that their advice would support him in his resolve. They counselled him to start for France at once. In his account of the incident he writes as follows of his wife's noble conduct:—

"My wife especially, whose courage and whose zeal for my honour and interests were not in the least abated by all her past sufferings, supplicated me to let no consideration of her or our children stand for a moment in the way of my engagements to our friends and my duty to my country, adding that she would answer for our family during my absence, and that the same Providence which had so often, as it were, miraculously preserved us would, she was confident, not desert us now."

Accordingly next morning he started off for Philadelphia and sought an interview with Adet, to whom he showed the letters of Keogh and Simms, informing him of the representative character of these men, and referring him to Hamilton Rowan as to the truth of his statement.

He found Adet now an ardent supporter of his design,

and was promised introductions to the French Government and even the expenses of his expedition. The former he accepted whilst refusing the offer of money, and the matter was definitely arranged.

Arthur, the sailor boy, was then called on to act as messenger to Ireland. He was ordered to communicate the news of Tone's journey to France to five persons in Ireland only. These were—In Belfast, Russell, Neilson, and Simms; in Dublin, Keogh and M'Cormick. To everyone else, even his parents, he was to say that Tone was settled on a farm at Princeton, in New Jersey. Arthur then embarked on board a ship called the Susannah, commanded by a Captain Baird, which was bound for Belfast, and, arriving safely, faithfully fulfilled his mission, though for long enough his brother heard no news of him.

After this Tone promptly settled his business affairs, leaving as much money as possible in the hands of his wife. Adet provided him with a letter of recommendation, in cypher, directed to the Committee of Public Safety, as the supreme governing body in France was then called.

One day in Philadelphia was spent with the latest arrived emigrant, who was no less a person than brave old Napper Tandy, of street ballad fame. After long hiding and adventures almost as thrilling as Hamilton Rowan's, he had arrived in America from Hamburg just in time to see Wolfe Tone and wish him luck in his mission. Tandy was to follow Tone to France not long after to play his part manfully in the drama of the year '98, and to suffer for it, too, if not the extreme penalty, yet enough to entitle him to honour and regard. Reynolds and Rowan Hamilton were along with Tone on this day which he spent with Napper Tandy in Philadelphia. Hamilton alone accompanied him when on the night of December 13th he arrived back at his home in Princeton to say a good-bye to his family. A festive supper had been prepared, and Tone had brought a few gifts for his wife, sister, and little ones. After supper Rowan Hamilton went away, not wishing to intrude upon the family circle in the hour of parting. But instead of indulging in expressions of grief, the heroic wife and sister sat with him far into the night talking with enthusiasm of the glorious enterprise on which he was bound. In remembering all that he accomplished for Ireland, we should remember, too, the woman who sent him back across the ocean to work for Ireland. Had he been wedded to a selfish and petulant, or even to a timid and helpless wife, his career of usefulness would have ended with his exile. On the 1st of January, 1796, he sailed from New York, and after a prosperous voyage landed safely at Havre de Grace.

Chapter X.

ENVOY TO FRANCE.

LANDING in France on the 2nd day of February, 1796, Wolfe Tone, ere that month, the shortest of the year, had ended, had laid the appeal of Ireland before the French Directory and chief military authorities, and had won from them a favourable response and promises of help. The whole story is told in the diary, which night after night he wrote, telling the history of each day's work for the woman far away who loved him. He knew so little French that travelling from Havre-de-Grace to Paris he was entirely dependent on a travelling companion to help him along; and yet it fell to him under such disadvantages to plead his country's cause—reason, dissuade, and advise as to the best means of helping her. His first influential friend in Paris was Munroe, the American Ambassador, to whom he presented himself two days after arrival (February 15th) with Adet's letter of recommendation. From

Munroe he received the address of the French Foreign Minister, Charles de la Croix, and, calling the same afternoon, saw him for a minute, and left his passport (drawn out in the name of James Smith) and Adet's letter. The next day he spent strolling round the city, viewing its principal sights. On February 17th he again called at the Foreign Office, and was informed by De la Croix that Adet's letter had been deciphered and sent before the Directoire Executive or Supreme Ministry of France; that the communication was considered of the utmost importance, and that he was to be put into touch with a person in the Foreign Office called Madgett, who was an Irishman, and who, knowing English and French, would be able to understand all information he had to give concerning Ireland. The Minister on this occasion treated him with great deference, and accompanied him to the door as he left. Tone's heart beat high as he noted this, the respect shown to him on account of his mission—it was an augury of success.

Madgett received him in most friendly fashion, having heard of him from Hamilton Rowan, and entered with great seriousness into the discussion of his business. At the outset we may state that Madgett, though friendly to Ireland, as was also General Clarke, another Franco-Irishman, proved a stumbling block in Tone's way. Each of these men had ideas and plans of their own, which were not founded on practical knowledge of the condition of the country. Instead of advocating Tone's suggestions, they were always trying to get his support and approval for their own. In the first conversation with Madgett, Tone explained in plain terms what he considered necessary as a basis of success. With a large force of 20,000 men or so sent as an invasion to Ireland instant success would attend the enterprise. If 5,000 were sent with arms enough for large bodies of the Irish, they would have to fight hard, but the whole country would assuredly waken up and rally to their aid, and ultimately overthrow the English. At his second interview Madgett told him the French Government had turned seriously to the consideration of Irish affairs; that they felt England was invulnerable, except through Ireland, and that they were ready to complete a treaty, offensive and defensive, with the latter country, and to send arms and money to her assistance. He urged an idea of his own, namely—that arms should be sent into Ireland via America, and said eighteen brass cannon had already been forwarded thence to Belfast. Tone strongly disapproved of this as likely to alarm the Government, and to create, when the Irish were armed, local riots which would have no good effect but to get the leaders into trouble. Day after day these consultations went on, and Tone was informed that the Ministry actually wished to recognise him as an Irish Ambassador, and intended to send an envoy to Ireland to bring back orders approving his appointment, so that he would be in a position of authority to arrange the Franco-Irish alliance. Tone was immensely flattered, but with sound commonsense pointed out that this course of action would put information into the possession of too many people in Ireland; that when a Government was created in Ireland it would be time enough to talk of embassies.

On February 22nd he called to give to Madgett a memorandum on the state of Ireland, to be laid before the Directory. He found his erewhile hopeful friend in a condition of despondency. The French navy was in a bad way, he said, and could not transport a large army to Ireland. 2,000 was the number of men talked of, but artillery and arms would be sent and money lent for the Irish to conduct a war themselves. Tone firmly insisted that 5,000 at the least would be needed to make the nucleus of an army; 2,000 would be as easily crushed as 20. Tone concluded his diary that night by sketching out in it the plan of revolution to be followed if no more than 5,000 men were sent.

"Suppose we get 5,000 men and 30,000, or even 20,000, stand of arms and a train of artillery, I conceive, in the first place, the embarkation must be from Holland, but in all events the landing must be in the North, as near Belfast as possible. Had we 20,000, or even 15,000, in the first instance, we should begin by the capital, the seizing of which would secure everything. With 5,000 we must proceed on an entirely revolutionary plan, I fear (that is to say, reckon only on the Sans-culottes), and if necessary put every man, horse, guinea, and potatoe in Ireland in requisition. I should also conceive that it would be our policy at first to avoid an action, supposing the Irish army stuck to the Government. Every day would strengthen and discipline us, and give us opportunity to work upon them. I doubt whether we could, until we had obtained some advantage in the field, frame any body that would venture to call itself an Irish Government, but if we could it would be of the best importance. '*Hang those who talk of fear.*' With *5,000* men and very strong measures we should ultimately succeed. The only difference between that number and 20,000 is that with the latter there would be no fighting, and with this we may have some hard knocks. . . Oh, good God, good God! What would I give to-night that we were safely landed and encamped on the Cavehill! If we can find our way so far, I think we shall puzzle John Bull to work us out. Surely we can do as much as the Chouans or the people of La Vendee."

The interesting point about this extract to readers of the present day is that Belfast is spoken of as a more suitable rebel rendezvous than Dublin, and as if the surrounding country were more in sympathy with the cause of Freedom.

A week and a day had now elapsed since Tone's first interview with the American Minister, Munroe. He now returned to report his progress, and to ask advice from one who seemed to him a true friend to Ireland and a wise and experienced diplomatist. He unburdened his mind to him freely regarding his negotiations with De la Croix and his subaltern and interpreter Madgett. Munroe advised him to go immediately to headquarters instead of negotiating entirely with subordinates. Tone mentioned Carnot, who was favourably known in Ireland, and who was said to speak

English. Munroe agreed that either Carnot or La Reveillière Lepaux should be instantly called upon. He explained that the time was favourable for the consideration of Irish affairs, as the French were greatly exasperated against England, and the members of the Directoire were fair-minded and just, not likely to aim at the conquest of Ireland, but certain to favour its liberation.

Tone then parted on most cordial terms with this friendly adviser, deciding to pluck up courage to visit Carnot the very next day. He was not a little agitated when considering the importance of the mission, and records his sense of his own unworthiness in his journal:—

"And now am I not a pretty fellow to go to the Directoire Executif? It is very singular that so obscure an individual should be thrown into such a situation. I presume I do not write those memorandums to flatter myself, and I here solemnly call God to witness the purity of my motives, and the uprightness with which I shall endeavour to carry myself through this arduous and critical situation. I hope I may not ruin a noble cause by any weakness or indiscretion of mine. As to my integrity, I can answer for myself."

Wolfe Tone's Appeal to France.

CONCLUSION OF THE MEMORIAL PRESENTED TO THE DIRECTORY, FEBRUARY, 1796.

I HAVE now done. I submit to the wisdom of the French Government that England is the implacable, inveterate, irreconcilable enemy of the Republic, which never can be in perfect security whilst that nation retains the dominion of the sea; that, in consequence, every possible effort should be made to humble her pride and to reduce her power; that it is in Ireland, *and in Ireland only*, that she is vulnerable—a fact of the truth of which the French Government cannot be too strongly impressed; that by establishing a free Republic in Ireland they attach to France a grateful ally, whose cordial assistance in peace and war she might command, and who, from situation and produce, could most essentially serve her; that at the same time they cut off from England her most firm support, in losing which she is laid under insuperable difficulties in recruiting her army, and especially in equipping, victualling, and manning her navy, which, unless for the resources she drew from Ireland, she would be absolutely unable to do; that by these means—and, suffer me to add, *by these means only*—her arrogance can be effectually humbled, and her enormous and increasing power at sea reduced within due bounds—an object essential, not only to France, but to all Europe; that it is at least possible, by the measures mentioned, that not only her future resources as to her navy may be intercepted and cut off at the fountain head, but that a part of her fleet may be actually transferred to the Republic of Ireland; that the Irish people are united and prepared and want but the means to begin; that, not to speak of the policy or the pleasure of revenge in humbling a haughty and implacable rival, it is in itself a great and splendid act of generosity and justice, worthy of the Republic, to rescue a whole nation from a slavery under which they have groaned for six hundred years; that it is for the glory of France, after emancipating Holland and receiving Belgium into her bosom, to establish one more free Republic in Europe; that it is for her interest to cut off for ever, as she now may do, one-half of the resources of England, and lay her under extreme difficulties in the employment of the other.

For all these reasons, in the name of justice, of humanity, of liberty, of my own country, and of France herself, I supplicate the Directory to take into consideration the state of Ireland; and by granting her the powerful aid and protection of the Republic, to enable her at once to vindicate her liberty, to humble her tyrant, and to assume that independent station among the nations of the earth for which her soil, her productions and her position, her population and her spirit have designed her.

Chapter XI.

INTERVIEW WITH CARNOT.

"*Et quand je vois, Carnot,*
Dicretant la Victoire;
Ah, je dis marquant le pas,
Comme autrefois la France est prête
Comme Autrefois.
French Military Chanson.

THE account of Tone's interview with Carnot must be given in the words of his diary as recorded under the date 24th February, 1796:—

"Went at twelve o'clock, in a fright, to the Luxembourg; conning speeches in execrable French all the way: What shall I say to Carnot? Well, '*whatsoever the Lord putteth in my mouth, that surely shall I utter.*' Plucked up a spirit as I drew near the palace, and mounted the stairs like a lion. Went into the first bureau that I found open, and demanded at once to see Carnot. The clerks stared a little, but I repeated my demand with a courage truly heroic; on which they instantly submitted, and sent a person to conduct me. This happened to be his day for giving audience, which each member of the Executive Directory does in his turn. Introduced by my guide into the ante-chamber, which was filled with people; the officers of state, all in their new costume. Write a line in English and delivered it to one of the Huissiers, stating that a stranger just arrived from America wished to speak to citizen Carnot on an affair of consequence. He brought me an answer in two minutes that I should have an audience. The folding doors were now thrown open, a bell being previously rung to give notice to the people, that all who had business might present themselves, and citizen Carnot appeared, in the *petit costume of* white satin with crimson robe, richly embroidered. It is very elegant, and resembles almost exactly the draperies of Van Dyke. He went round the room receiving papers and answering those who addressed him. I told my friend the Huissier, in marvellous French, that my business was too important to be transacted there, and that I would return on another day, when it would not be Carnot's turn to give audience, and when I should hope to find him at leisure. He mentioned this to Carnot, who ordered me instantly to be shown into an inner apartment, and that he would see me as soon as the audience was over. That, I thought, looked well, and began accordingly to con my speech again. In the apartment were five or six personages, who being, like myself, of great distinction, were admitted to a private audience. I allowed them all precedence, as I wished to have my will of Carnot, and while they were in their turns speaking with him, I could not help reflecting how often I had wished for the opportunity I then enjoyed; what schemes I had laid, what hazards I had run; when I looked round and saw myself actually in the cabinet of the Executive Directory, *vis-à-vis* citizen Carnot, the *Organiser of Victory*, I could hardly believe my own senses, and felt as if it were all a dream. However, I was not in the least degree disconcerted, and when I presented myself, after the rest were dismissed, I had all my faculties, such as they were, as well at my command as on any occasion in my life. Why do I mention those trifling circumstances? It is because they will not be trifling in her eyes, for whom they were written. I began the discourse by saying, in horrible French, that I had been informed he spoke English. 'A little, sir; but I perceive you speak French, and if you please, we will converse in that language.' I answered, still in my jargon, that if he could have the patience to endure me, I would endeavour, and only prayed him to stop me whenever I did not make myself understood. I then told him I was an Irishman; that I had been Secretary and Agent to the Catholics of that country, who were about 3,000,000 of people; that I was also in perfect possession of the sentiments of the Dissenters, who were at least 900,000, and that I wished to communicate with him on the actual state of Ireland. He stopped me here to express a doubt as to the numbers being so great as I represented. I answered a calculation had been made within these few years, grounded on the number of houses, which was ascertained for purposes of revenue; that, by that calculation, the people of Ireland amounted to 4,100,000, and it was acknowledged to be considerably under the truth. He seemed a little surprised at this, and I proceeded to state that the sentiments of all those people were unanimous in favour of France, and eager to throw off the yoke of England. He asked me then 'What they wanted.' I said, 'An armed force in the commencement, for a *point d'appui*, until they could organise themselves, and undoubtedly a supply of arms and some money.' I added that I had already delivered in a memorial on the subject to the Minister of Foreign Relations, and that I was preparing another, which would explain to him, in detail, all that I knew on the subject, better than I could in conversation. He then said, 'We shall see those memorials.' The Organiser of Victory proceeded to ask me, 'Were there not some strong places in Ireland?' I answered I knew of none, but some works to defend the harbour of Cork. He stopped me here, saying, 'Aye, Cork! But may it not be necessary to land there?' By which I had perceived that he had been *organising* a little already, in his own mind. I answered, I thought not. That if a landing in *force* were attempted, it would be better near the capital, for obvious reasons; if with a small army, it should be in the North, rather than the South of Ireland, for reasons which he would find in my memorials. He then asked me, 'Might there not be some danger or delay in a longer navigation?' I answered it would not make a difference of two days, which was nothing in comparison of the advantages. I then told him that I came to France by direction and concurrence of the men, who (and here I was at a loss for a French word, with which, seeing my embarrassment, he supplied me) *guided* the two great parties I had mentioned. This satisfied me clearly that he attended to and understood me. I added, that I had presented myself in August last, in Philadelphia, to citizen Adet, and delivered to him such credentials as I had with me; that he did not at that juncture think it advisable for me to come in person, but offered to transmit a memorial, which I accordingly delivered to him. That about the end of November last, I received letters from my friends in Ireland, repeating their instructions in the strongest manner, that I should, if possible, force my way to France, and lay the situation of Ireland before its Government. That, in consequence, I had again waited on citizen Adet, who seemed eager to assist me, and offered me a letter to the Directoire Exécutif, which I accepted with gratitude. That I sailed from America in the very first vessel, and was arrived about a fortnight; that I had delivered my letter to the Minister of Foreign Affairs, who had ordered me to explain myself without reserve to citizen Madgett, which I had accordingly done. That by his advice I had prepared and delivered one memorial, on the actual state of Ireland, and was then at work on another, which would comprise the whole of the subject. That I had the highest respect for the Minister, and that as to Madgett, I had no reason whatsoever to doubt him, but, nevertheless, must be permitted to say that, in my mind, it was a business of too great importance to be transacted with a mere *Commis.* That I should not think I had discharged my duty, either to France or Ireland, if I left any measure unattempted which might draw the attention of the Directory to the situation of the latter country; and that, in consequence, I had presumed to present myself to him, and to implore his attention to the facts contained in my two memorials. That I would also presume to request that, if any doubt or difficulty arose in his mind on any of those facts, he would have the goodness to permit me to explain. I concluded by saying that I looked upon it as a favourable omen that I had been allowed to communicate with him, as he was already perfectly well known by reputation in Ireland, and was the very man of whom my friends had spoken. He shook his head and smiled, as if he doubted me a little. I assured him the fact was so; and, as a proof, told him that in Ireland we all knew, three years ago, that he could speak English; at which he did not seem displeased. I then rose, and after the usual apologies, took my leave; but I had not cleared the ante-chamber, when I recollected a very material circumstance, which was, that I had not told him, in fact, *who*, but merely *what* I was; I was, therefore, returning on my steps, when I was stopped by the sentry, demanding my card, but from this dilemma I was extricated by my lover the Huissier, and again admitted. I then told Carnot that, as to my situation, credit, and the station, I had filled in Ireland, I begged leave to refer him to James Monroe, the American Ambassador. He seemed struck with this, and then for the first time real one and that under which I travelled and was described in my passport. I then took a slip of paper, and wrote the name 'James Smith, citoyen Americain,' and under it 'Theobald Wolfe Tone,' which I handed him, adding that my real name was the undermost. He took the paper, and looking over it, said, 'Ha! Theobald Wolfe Tone,' with the expression of one who has just recollected a circumstance, from which little movement I augur good things. I then told him I would finish my memorial as soon as possible, and hoped he would permit me, in the course of a few days after, to present myself again to him; to which he answered, 'By all means;' and so I again took my leave. Here is a full and true account of my first audience of the Executive Directory of France, in the person of citizen Carnot, the organiser of victory. I think I came off very clear. What am I to think of all this? As yet I have met no difficulty nor check, nothing to discourage me, but I wish with such extravagant passion for the emancipation of my country, and I do so abhor and detest the very name of England, that I doubt my own judgment, lest I see things in too favourable a light. I hope I am doing my duty. It is a bold measure; after all if it should succeed, and my visions be realised—Huzza! *Vive la République!* I am a pretty fellow to negotiate with the Directory of France, pull down a monarchy and establish a republic; to break a connection of 600 years' standing and contract a fresh alliance with another country. '*By'r Lakin, a parlous fear.*' What would my old friend Fitzgibbon say if he was to read those memorandums? '*He called me dog before he had a cause.*' I remember he used to say that I was a viper in the bosom of Ireland. Now that I am in Paris, I will venture to say that he lies, and that I am a better Irishman than he and his whole gang of rascals, as well as the gang who are opposing him *as it were.* But this is all castle-building. Let me finish my memorial and deliver it to the Minister.—Nothing but *Minister and Directoires Exécutif and revolutionary memorials*. Well, my friend Plunket (but I sincerely forgive him), and my friend Magee, whom I have not yet forgiven, would not speak to me in Ireland, because I was a Republican. Sink or swim, I stand to-day on as high ground as either of them. My venerable friend, old Captain Russell, always had hopes of me in the worst of times. Huzza! I would give five louis d'ors for one day's conversation with P.P. What shall I do for want of his advice and assistance. Not but what I think I am doing pretty well, considering I am quite alone, with no papers, no one to consult or advise with, and shocking all Christian ears with the horrible jargon which I speak, and which is properly no language. I see I have grand diplomatic talents, and by and by I hope to have an opportunity of displaying my military ones, and showing that I am equally great in the cabinet and the field. This is sad stuff! except for my love, who will laugh at it, or P. P., who will enjoy it. I have to add to this day's journal, that I saw yesterday at the Luxembourg, besides my friend Carnot, the citizens Letourneur, the President, Barras, and La Reveilliere Lepaux. Barras looks like a soldier, and put me something in mind of James Bramston. La Reveilliere is extremely like Dr. Kearney. Mem.: I saw two *poissardes* admitted to speak to Carnot, who gave them money, whilst a general officer in his uniform was obliged to wait for his turn. Oh Lord! Oh Lord! shall I ever get to finish my memorial? But when I begin to write those ingenious memorandums, I feel just as if I were chatting with my dearest love, and know not when to leave off. By the by, there is a good deal of vanity in this day's journal. No matter, there is no one to know it, and I believe that wiser men, if they would speak the truth, would feel a little elevated in my situation; hunted from my own country as a traitor, living obscurely in America as an exile, and received in France, by the Executive Directory, almost as an Ambassador! Well, murder will out. I am as vain as the devil; and one thing which makes me wish so often for P. P. (not to mention the benefit of his advice) is to communicate with him the pleasure I feel at my present situation. I know how sincerely he would enjoy it, and also how he would plume himself on his own discernment, for he always foretold great things. So he did, sure enough; but will they be verified? Well, if all this be not vanity, I should be glad to know what it is. But nobody is the wiser, and so I will go finish my memorial. Sings, '*Allons, enfants de la patrie*,' &c."

Chapter XII.

HOPE DEFERRED.

"*Hope long deferred*," saith the Scripture, "*maketh the heart of man sick.*" *I am sure mine just now is not in rude health. But I am sworn never to despair; so courage! Allons.*—*Wolfe Tone's Diary, June, 1796.*

TONE, within the very brief period which had elapsed since his landing, had completely fulfilled his mission. For several months following his interview with Carnot, he was left in a state of sickening suspense and uncertainty as to what the result was to be. His communications were kept up constantly with the Directoire through the medium of General Clarke, a person of importance in the War Department, who was of Irish extraction, and spoke English. Carnot put Tone in the hands of Clarke, just as De la Croix had put him in touch with Madgett, and from these two go-betweens he received the most contradictory accounts of what was going on.

Madgett assumed the air of knowing everything, and had

his own ideas as to how to carry on the campaign against England. For one favourite scheme he was constantly asking Tone's co-operation, namely—to recruit Irish prisoners of war, liberate them, and send them to Ireland to prepare the people for revolt, and also back to the English fleet to weaken it by mutiny.

Tone was aggravated beyond measure by these proposals, as he well knew the safety of the Irish leaders and the success of the revolt depended above all things on the French invasion coming as a complete surprise to England. Again and again he argued against these dangerous schemes, and departed thinking he had convinced their advocates; but always found them revived on his return. The Directoire also desired to have more recent information as to the condition of Ireland than that brought by Tone, and arranged to send an envoy to the country. Tone urged in vain that no essential change could have taken place since his departure, and that his information was sufficiently up to date, that the risk would not be worth the slight advantage gained by such a proceeding.

General Clarke irritated and puzzled him more than anyone else. He had his own theories and ideas about Ireland, being himself of Irish extraction, and had visited Ireland before the recent Republican fervour set in. He suggested, among other things, that the aristocracy of the country might be led to take part in the revolution, and mentioned the names of the Earl of Ormond and Lord Chancellor Fitzgibbon as probable supporters. He refused to believe that the Irish would be favourable to a Republic; wanted to know if the Catholics would not elect one of their chiefs as King; and later on inserted in a proclamation intended for distribution in Ireland an announcement that if Ireland was still devoted to the House of Stuart a member of that family could be found. Tone had these monarchical expressions erased from the proclamation; but to the very last Clarke kept harping on this string, even suggesting that Tone himself might be chosen King. He also worried Tone to write a manifesto to be promulgated among the Radicals and Republicans in England, and hinted to him that an attempt would be made to stir up revolution there.

During these months of spring, whilst Tone was working and wearying in Paris, the French army in Italy was achieving wonderful successes, which are recorded in the diary with this note:—" The French general is Buonaparte, a Corsican." Tone, though he knew it not, was watching the uprising of a wonderful luminary, whose fiery career was to astonish Europe within a very few years, and who was to prove a baleful star in regard to its influence on the destinies of Ireland. To add to his troubles and perplexities, Tone's funds ran so low that he was on the verge of being penniless. As we shall see, his financial difficulties were relieved by his being made an officer in the French service; but during this period of probation he was forced to be constantly considering his expenditure and living as modestly as possible. He made no friends or acquaintances outside the circle of those with whom his mission brought him into contact. At the theatre and in attending the military spectacles of the French capital, he strove to lighten those waiting hours; but when the scene was gayest his heart was full of lonely yearnings for the dear ones far away, without whose presence no enjoyment was complete and no real happiness possible. At every important crisis he longed for the company of his comrade, Tom Russell, to rejoice with him when things looked prosperous, to advise him at times of difficulty. Nothing more deeply affected him than a martial display. Tears gushed to his eyes when he saw the soldiers of France under arms, and thought of what they could do for Ireland. At the end of May he was present, and given a place of honour among the foreign representatives, at a *Fête des Victoires*, held in honour of the successes in Italy. The ceremony took place in the *Champ de Mars,* where a great statue of Liberty was erected. Odes were chanted, and Carnot presented to every regiment a banner and garland of oak. As Tone stood there and watched the stalwart grenadiers receive the standards from the hands of the Organiser of Victory, he was strangely affected. Tears coursed down his cheeks, the outcome of repressed emotion and tortured and deferred hope. He thought of Ireland over the sea and of brave men waiting there for those banners of France to be unfurled on the breeze; for arms to be brought to their shores and placed in their hands, that were ready and pledged to strike in Freedom's battle.

But whilst Tone, tortured by uncertainty, sadly viewed the stirring military festival, away in Switzerland envoys of importance had arrived from Ireland with news which confirmed all that he had said, and were demanding to be put in communication with a representative of the French Republic.

One of these envoys from Ireland was none other than Lord Edward Fitzgerald, who had at the beginning of that year been brought into the United Irish organisation. He was the youngest brother of the Duke of Leinster, and had seen service in the British army in America. Had Wolfe Tone's boyish ambition been gratified, and had he been allowed to go off to the wars instead of to Trinity College, possibly these two would have met. As it was, they were but slightly acquainted.

From his letters to his mother, written from Canada during his soldier years, it will be seen that Fitzgerald was a born Republican; an ardent lover of freedom; simple in his tastes and habits. A visit to Paris brought Fitzgerald into touch with the revolutionists, and led him to renounce his title and become an advanced Republican. In Irish politics he had always been on the popular side, and as a member of the Irish House of Commons he opposed the

Gunpowder and Convention Bills, measures which aimed at making impossible, gatherings like those of the Volunteers. In the year '94, when Wolfe Tone was active in Ireland, Fitzgerald was living with his young French wife, Pamela, daughter of Philip of Orleans, in a cottage at Frescati, Co. Kildare. In May, 1796, accompanied by Arthur O'Connor, he embarked from London to Hamburg, and leaving his wife there, proceeded to Bale, in Switzerland. Here the two envoys put themselves in the hands of the French Ambassador, and expressed their desire to travel to Paris and communicate in person with members of the Directory.

Barthelemy, the French Ambassador, communicated their desire to Charles de la Croix, and in consequence, General Hoche, who, though Tone did not yet know, was already appointed commander of the French expedition to Ireland, was sent to Switzerland to interview O'Connor. On account of his marriage with Pamela, Fitzgerald was excluded from this interview lest it should be imagined that the interests of the House of Orleans were under discussion.

O'Connor's information proved that Republican fervour and the United Irish organisation had spread since Tone left Ireland. Hoche came away from the interview more desirous than ever of attacking England through Ireland.

On his return to Paris in about a month, he immediately sought out Wolfe Tone, who had in the meantime been made an officer in the French army, with the rank of *Chef de Brigade*, and a salary sufficient to relieve his financial difficulties.

The acquaintance with General Hoche opens a brighter era in the history of our era. From this day he was no longer under the necessity of going backwards and forwards from Clarke to Madgett to get a hint of what was going forward, but was in the full confidence of the brilliant young general chosen for the command in Ireland.

Chapter XIII.

HOCHE THE FRIEND OF IRELAND.

DURING the month of May, as we see from his diary, Tone's hopes had been at the lowest ebb. In June the arrangements for his post in the French army cheered him up, though constantly we find him checking his tendency to be sanguine, and writing that he will not allow himself to exult till he is actually under canvas with French invaders on Irish soil. On the 28th June he had an interview with Clarke, who was in possession of a paper giving information about the spread of the United Irish organisation in Ireland. He showed it to Tone, who did not recognise the handwriting, and otherwise excited his curiosity, but told him nothing of Hoche's interview with Arthur O'Connor. However, he spoke of the invasion as definitely settled, Hoche being the appointed commander; he spoke as if he, too, intended to be of the party. The diary of that day is somewhat exultant, as the following quotation will show:—

"Eighteen months ago it was a million to one that I should be hanged as a traitor, and now I am likely to enter the country in which I was not thought worthy to live, at the head of a regiment of horse. It is singular, P. P. used always to be foretelling great things and I never believed him; yet a part of his prophecy seems likely to be verified. My name may be spoken of yet, and I trust there is nothing thus far attached to it of which I need be ashamed. If ever I come to be a great man, let me never forget two things—the honour of my masters of the General Committee, who refused to sacrifice me to the requisition of Mr. Grattan; and the friendship, I may say, of the whole town of Belfast in the moment of my departure to exile. These are two instances of steadiness of spirit under circumstances peculiarly trying, which do honour to them, to me, and to our common nature."

July 1st he opens with this record:—" Sings with great courage, '*July the first in Oldbridge town there was a grievous battle.*' We made no great figure that day, that is the God's truth of it. Well, no matter! What's past's past. We must see and do better the next time; besides, we pulled up a little the year after at Aughrim, and made a most gallant defence at Limerick. But I am writing a history of the wars in Ireland instead of minding my business."

On July 12th came a turning point in his fortunes. As he sat in his cabinet studying tactics, and remembering that it was the anniversary of Aughrim, a dragoon entered and summoned him to General Clarke's house. He went there and waited, when, "at three o'clock" he relates:—"The door opened and a very handsome, well-made young fellow in a brown coat and nankeen pantaloons entered, and said, " Vous étes le citoyen Smith?" Tone took him for a War Office clerk, and responded briefly in the affirmative. The stranger added that he believed he was also called Wolfe Tone, and announced himself as General Hoche. The afternoon was spent in discussing the risks and prospects of the Irish invasion, and finally they came to the point which the French seem to have always been sceptical of, namely—Ireland's Republicanism.

Tone assured him that he knew of no one in Ireland who would dream of a monarchy, and suspected that General Clarke had been instilling some of his old-fashioned ideas into the young general's head.

They then adjourned to Carnot's apartments, where Tone was invited for the first time to dine. Carnot joined them with a pocket map of Ireland, and the talk was all of the expedition. Tone said little, but listened. In his diary he concludes his account of the day's proceedings thus:—

"This was a grand day. I dined with the President of the Executive Directory of France, beyond all comparison the most illustrious station in Europe. I am very proud of it, because it has come fairly in the line of my duty, and I have made no unworthy sacrifice to obtain it. I like Carnot extremely, and Hoche, I think, yet better."

So ended the first twelfth of July which Wolfe Tone had spent ashore since he left Ireland.

On July 23rd, Hoche informed him that he was making Rennes his headquarters, and that he (Tone) was to live incognito at a village near, to be at hand for consultation, and ready to embark. On this occasion Hoche inquired what part men of property in Ireland might be expected to take. Tone answered that their opposition was to be reckoned on. Hoche, who had met Arthur O'Connor, and been in touch with Lord Edward Fitzgerald, mentioned these gentlemen.

Tone immediately praised them, and acknowledged that they were exceptional, and likely to be of the patriot party. Hoche and Tone then agreed that it would be important to guard against anything like massacre or unnecessary bloodshed. "Guillotine a man," said the French Republican, "and you get rid of an individual, it is true; but you make all his friends and connections your enemies for ever." This appreciation of Hoche then follows:—

"I am heartily glad to find Hoche of this humane temperament, because I hope I am humane myself, and trust we shall be able to prevent unnecessary bloodshed in Ireland. He then desired me to call on him every two or three days at seven o'clock, at which I might be sure to find him disengaged, adding that he did not wish to mix me with the crowd, and after several expressions of civility and attention on his part, all which I set down to the credit of my country, we parted. I like Hoche more and more. He is one of the finest fellows I ever conversed with, with a fine manly mind and a fine manly figure."

So commenced a friendship which through a brief period of common anxiety and adversity was to endure between the young French general and the Irish envoy.

Chapter XIV.

" THE FRENCH ARE ON THE SEA."

ONE left Paris in the middle of September for Rennes, saying good-bye to his most intimate acquaintances, Madgett, his nephew Sullivan, and Aherne, the only Irish resident of Paris with whom he had at this time associated. Duckett, another Irishman resident in the French capital, on the pretext of political business, he had always refused to recognise, having suspicions of his honesty. At Rennes his chief friend was Colonel Shee, an old Irish officer, uncle to General Clarke. With this veteran he was in constant consultation as to plans of action and routes to be taken in Ireland. He also confided to him much of his private affairs and anxieties, and entrusted him with the charge of appealing to the French Government on behalf of his family, if he should happen to fall in action. He had arranged for his wife and children and sister to come to France, and at the very time that he was in Bantry Bay in December they made the voyage. All this time General Hoche, who was anxious to push forward the Irish expedition, was hampered by difficulties and objections advanced by the Marine Department. At the end of October, Tone heard of the arrest of his friends Russell, Nielson, Sampson, and others, and his impatience waxed uncontrollable. On October 30th, he arrived at

Brest, where the preparations for embarkation were tardily progressing. Hoche at length succeeded in having the admiral, Villaret Joyeuse, replaced by one more favourable to the expedition, Admiral de Galles, and at length, on December 1st, Tone went on board the Indomitable, all the troops being shipped and the vessels munitioned. Even at this late stage in the proceedings delays occurred, and it was December 16th before they at last sailed. The fleet on leaving Brest included seventeen sail of the line, thirteen frigates, seven corvettes, and six transports—in all, forty-three vessels—with troops to the number of over 13,000 on board. There was also a supply of arms and artillery to put in the hands of the Irish insurgents on landing. Hoche had kept faith with Tone. The invasion was in all respects the most formidable that had ever threatened England. Ireland, too, was well prepared to support it. The men who rose and fought in '98 were ready in '96, and others, like brave Lord Edward, who were to die or pass into prison before the rising, were at this earlier era waiting for the ships of France, and eager to take the field. Had the landing been effected we cannot doubt that insurrection would have burst forth all over the country. It cost England time and trouble in '98 to quell the separate risings of Ulster, Leinster, and the West. If in '96 she had found herself face to face with simultaneous risings, could she have grappled with a French invasion of such magnitude? No; the peasants of Ireland, armed and aided by France, would have fulfilled the hopes of Tone and the United men by establishing in this green isle of the west a free Republican Nation.

But the day of God's deliverance for Ireland was not yet. The storm winds saved England from the overthrow which all her forces in Ireland could not have prevented; and Wolfe Tone's year of striving and contriving, his absence from his dear ones, his solitary nights and days through the long year that was now closing were to seem as if spent in vain.

On the very day of sailing the squadron was separated in a fog, and though several of the lost ships afterwards rejoined the main body, the *Fraternité* was amongst the number of those which was never again sighted. Its absence was fatal to the expedition, as the Admiral de Galles and the commander-in-chief, General Hoche, were on board it, and in their absence Grouchy (second in command of the military) and the other admirals, though urged by Tone, would not take upon them the responsibility of effecting a landing.

We shall quote here from the Diary:—

"December 22nd. This morning, at eight, we have neared Bantry Bay considerably, but the fleet is terribly scattered; no news of the *Fraternité*; I believe it is the first instance of an admiral in a clean frigate with moderate weather and moonlight night parting company with his fleet. . . All rests now upon Grouchy, and I hope he may turn out well; he has a glorious game in his hands, if he has spirits and talents to play it. If he succeeds it will immortalise him. I do not at all like the countenance of the *Etat Major* at this crisis. When they speak of the expedition, it is in a style of despondency, and when they are not speaking of it, they are playing cards and laughing; they are every one brave of their persons, but I see nothing of that spirit of enterprise combined with a steady resolution which the present situation demands. They stared at me this morning when I said that Grouchy was the man in the whole army who had least reason to regret the absence of the general, and began to talk of responsibilities and difficulties as if any great enterprise was without responsibilities and difficulties. I was burning with rage; however, I said nothing, and will say nothing till I get ashore, if ever I am so happy as to arrive there. We are gaining the Bay by slow degrees with a head wind at east, where is has hung these five weeks. To-night we hope, if nothing extraordinary happens, to cast anchor in the mouth of the Bay, and work up to-morrow morning. These delays are dreadful to my impatience. I am now so near the shore that I can see distinctly two old castles, yet I am utterly uncertain whether I shall ever set foot on it. . . . . At half-past six cast anchor off Bere Island, being still four leagues from our landing place. At work with General Cherin writing and translating proclamations, &c., all our printed papers, including my two pamphlets, being on board the *Fraternité*, which is pleasant.

"December 23rd. Last night it blew a heavy gale from the eastward, with snow, so that the mountains are covered this morning, which will render our bivouacs extremely amusing. . . . In consequence, we are this morning separated for the fourth time; sixteen sail, including nine or ten of the line, with Baudet and Grouchy, are at anchor with us, and about twenty are blown out to sea; luckily the gale set from the shore, so I am in hopes no mischief may ensue after. I am sick to the very soul of this suspense.

(On this day Tone proposed to the Generals that he should be given leave to go ashore himself with a legion and some light artillery with any officers who might volunteer to accompany him. A Council of War was called for the next day to consider this proposal and the situation generally. The Council of War, held December 24th, decided to urge Grouchy to land with the remnants of the army. In consequence Tone's spirits revived, and the record in his diary is full of hope.)

"December 24th. . . . I must do Grouchy the justice to say that the moment we gave our opinion in favour of proceeding he took his part decidedly and like a man of spirit; he instantly set about preparing the *ordre de bataille*, and we finished it without delay. We are not 6,500 strong, but they are tried soldiers, who have seen fire, and I have

the strongest hopes that after all, we shall bring our enterprise to a glorious termination. It is a bold attempt and truly original. All the time we were preparing the *ordre de bataille* we were laughing immoderately at the poverty of our means, and I believe under the circumstances, it was the merriest council of war that was ever held. . . .
. . . It is altogether an enterprise truly *unique;* we have not a guinea; we have not a tent; we have not a horse to draw our four pieces of artillery; the general-in-chief marches on foot; we leave all our baggage behind us; we have nothing but the arms in our hands, the clothes on our backs, and a good courage; but that is sufficient. With all these original circumstances, such as I believe never were found united in an expedition of such magnitude as that we are about to attempt, we are all as gay as larks. . . . We purpose to make a race for Cork as if the devil were in our bodies, and when we are fairly there, we will stop for a day or two to take breath and look about. . . . . . Well, I have worked hard to-day, not to speak of my boating party aboard the admiral, against wind and tide and in a rough sea. I have written and copied fifteen letters, beside these memorandums; pretty well for one day.

(Owing to the loss of printed proclamations which were on board the *Fraternité* with Hoche, Tone was obliged to write new proclamations and have a number of written copies made, and in the middle of all his anxiety helped at this clerk's work himself. This was the happiest, most hopeful day of the voyage. Next day the cloud of gloom again descended. The storm rose and prevented their carrying out their plan of landing.)

"December 25th. These memorandums are a strange mixture. Sometimes I am in preposterously high spirits, and at other times I am as dejected, according to the posture of our affairs. Last night I had the strongest expectations that to-day we should debark, but at two this morning

I was awakened by the wind. I rose immediately, and wrapping myself in my great coat, walked for an hour in the gallery, devoured by the most gloomy reflections. The wind continues right ahead, so that it is absolutely impossible to work up to the landing place, and God knows when it will change. The same wind is exactly favourable to bring the English upon us, and these cruel delays give the enemy time to assemble his entire force in this neighbourhood. . . . . Had we been able to land the first day and march directly to Cork, we should have infallibly carried it by a *coup de main*, and then we should have a footing in the country; but as it is, if we are taken, my fate will not be a mild one; the best I can expect is to be shot as an *émigré rentré*, unless I have the good fortune to be killed in the action; for most assuredly if the enemy will have us, he must fight for us. Perhaps I may be reserved for a trial, for the sake of striking terror into others, in which case I shall be hanged as a traitor and embowelled, &c. As to the embowelling, '*Je m'en fiche*,' if ever they hang me, they are welcome to embowel me if they please. These are pleasant prospects! Nothing on earth could sustain me now but the consciousness that I am engaged in a just and righteous cause. . . . . In this desperate state of affairs I propose to Cherin to sally out with all our forces to mount the Shannon, and, disembarking the troops, make a forced march to Limerick, which is probably unguarded, the garrison being, I am pretty certain, on its march to oppose us here, to pass the river at Limerick, and by forced marches push to the North.

(This suggestion was thought well of, but owing to the storm they could not communicate with the admiral and general, who were on another vessel. Tone concluded his Christmas Day diary with reflections of utter despair.)

"I see nothing before me, unless a miracle be wrought in our favour, but the ruin of the expedition, the slavery of my country, and my own destruction. Well, if I am to fall, at least I will sell my life as dear as individual resistance can make it. So now I have made up my mind. I have a merry Christmas of it to-day."

On December 27th the last gleam of hope shone forth and disappeared. The ships were ordered to sea with a view to their attempting to enter the Shannon. The storm made this impracticable, and there was nothing for it but to turn back to the French coast.

Chapter XV.

IN GERMANY AND HOLLAND.

SO ended the greatest invasion that had threatened England since the Armada. Tone could now only think of his wife and children, who had passed through that same terrible storm on their way to Europe. He dared not hope that France would launch another fleet, and, indeed, he feared that he would be discredited for having urged them to this enterprise, which had ended in such a *fiasco*. He resigned himself to the thought of living quietly and obscurely, being satisfied that he had not failed in his duty to his country.

"I hope," he wrote, "the Directory will not dismiss me the service for this unhappy failure, in which, certainly, I have nothing personally to reproach myself with; and in that case I shall be rich enough to live as a peasant. If God Almighty sends me my dearest love and darling babies in safety, I will buy or rent a little spot, and have done with the world for ever. I shall neither be great nor famous, nor powerful, but I may be happy."

The tenderness and real goodness of the great patriot's

character is shown by such passages as this. There is one incident in connection with this expedition which throws additional light on this side of his character. When given his military command, before starting he had to employ a servant, and instead of taking anyone who would have been of use to him, he chose a little boy, a soldier's son of Irish extraction, whom he found among the prisoners of war. The child was too young to be of any use to him more than to brush his coat and look after his portmanteau. However, he dressed him up finely and engaged him, giving this as his reason:—" He was an orphan and half naked." A dignitary of the Church who recently stigmatised Wolfe Tone as "an Atheistical coxcomb," would do well to consider this one little incident in the light of the standard which Holy Writ tells us will be adopted by the Judge of all—" I was in prison and ye visited me; naked and ye clothed me; and inasmuch as ye did it to the least of these my little ones ye did it unto me." Had Tone been a "coxcomb," he would assuredly have engaged a valet, who would have had some skill in adorning him; but here we see he thought more of dressing this little lad because he was " an orphan and half naked." In the same passage (Diary, November 23rd, '96) the charge of Atheism is as plainly refuted, when, expressing his anxiety as to the fate of his family should he fall in action, he writes:—

" I rely on the goodness of Providence, which has often interposed to save us; on the courage and prudence of my wife, and on the friendship of my brother to protect them. My darling babies! I dote on them. I feel the tears gush into my eyes whenever I think on them. I repeat to myself a thousand times the last words I heard from their innocent little mouths. God Almighty bless and protect them."

On December 20th, Matilda Tone, with her three children, and Mary, her sister-in-law, arrived at Hamburg. On the voyage a young Swiss merchant had formed an attachment for Mary, and wrote asking Tone's consent to his marriage. These letters, whilst most welcome, threw Tone into terrible anxiety about his wife, whose already delicate health had been shattered by that stormy voyage across the Atlantic. He appealed to Hoche for leave to go immediately to Hamburg, and was very kindly treated by the young general, who said he might be sent to Hamburg on a political mission, and who assured him at the same time that, though the expedition to Ireland was out of the question for the present, that when the enterprise was resumed he would be ready as ever to undertake it.

Old Colonel Shee likewise encouraged him, and gave an account of the dreadful experiences they had on board the *Fraternité*, which had been beating up and down the channel for a whole month, trying to avoid the English, separated from the rest of the fleet, and prevented by the storm from approaching the coast of Ireland.

Hoche in a letter of Remonstrance to the Directory gave it as his opinion that Grouchy should have landed without him. In departing to take command in Central Europe, Hoche did not abandon his intention of aiding Ireland, but wrote from the banks of the Rhine to this effect:—

"Should fortune lead me, as I trust it will, with this army to the gates of Vienna, I would still leave it to go to Dublin and from thence to London."

On the departure of Hoche, the Directory carried into effect one of those plans which Tone had constantly urged against. A plundering party was sent over to England to the number of 1,500 men. After a brief and ridiculous campaign, they were all captured by a body of militia and shut up in Pembroke Castle.

In April we find Tone with Hoche on the banks of the Rhine, strolling through Bonn, Cologne, and other German cities; but always pleading for leave to go on that mission to Hamburg in order to join his wife and children. At length, on April 20th, he departed, travelling by night and day. His journey brought him through Holland, and having written to appoint a place of meeting with his wife, he spent some time in seeing the sights of Amsterdam, and in investigating the military resources and methods of government of the recently founded Batavian Republic. The members of the Dutch Republican Parliament or Convention he describes as " plain, respectable looking men, who put me in mind of my old and ever respected masters of the general committee." The subject under discussion on the day he attended the Convention was whether the Government should or should not pay the clergy. He noticed a priest and several Protestant ministers among the members, but was informed by the Dutchman who introduced him that the clergy were to be later excluded from sitting in the House. Commenting on his visit to the Convention, he compared it and other legislative bodies to the much vaunted Irish Parliament of his own time in these words:—

" I have now seen the Parliament of Ireland, the Parliament of England, the Congress of the United States of America, the Corps Legislatif of France, and the Convention Batave; I have likewise seen our shabby Volunteer Convention of 1783, and the General Committee of the Catholics in 1793; so that I have seen in the way of deliberative bodies as many, I believe, as most men; and of all those I have mentioned, beyond all comparison the most shameless, profligate, and abandoned by all sense of virtue and principle, or even common decency, was the Legislature of my own unfortunate country. The scoundrels, I lose my temper every time I think of them."

Such was Wolfe Tone's opinion of Grattan's Parliament.

The political news which reached Tone in Holland was of the utmost importance, namely—that there was a mutiny of the British fleet at the Nore; that the French had signed a peace with the Emperor of Austria (thus putting an end to Hoche's campaign), and that the province of Ulster was being plundered and disarmed.

On May 7th he was at length re-united to his wife and family, and having conducted them through Holland and Belgium, sent them on to settle in Paris, and set out to join Hoche in Germany.

Chapter XVI.

WITH THE DUTCH REPUBLICANS.

OLFE TONE'S relations with the Dutch Republic of that day will have an additional interest for us, because, though the Dutch of Europe have relapsed to the Monarchical rule, a Dutch Republic is to-day in existence in South Africa, and has apparently inherited the anti-English policy that inspired the Government of the Hague to fit out an expedition for the invasion of Ireland.

We left Tone on his way to join Hoche, which he did at Friedburg, about June 10th. On the twelfth day of the same month Hoche sent for Tone, and informed him that an envoy from the United Irishmen had arrived to urge another expedition. This envoy was Lewines, a Dublin solicitor, a former acquaintance of Tone's. Tone went off to meet Lewines at Neuwied, and, coming with him to Coblenz on June 21st to take council with Hoche, they were informed that the Batavian Republic was projecting an expedition; a letter, in fact, from the Batavian Government asked Hoche to come secretly to the Hague, and to bring the Irish envoy.

On June 27th, Tone and Lewines went by appointment to the theatre at La Hague, and met Hoche, who was *incognito*. They accompanied him to his inn, and were informed that Governor-General Daendels and Admiral de Winter were anxious to achieve some great military success in order to raise the prestige of their young Republic, and were favourable to an expedition against British rule in Ireland. Hoche at first claimed on behalf of his own Government that the French and Dutch should go as allies; but seeing that they were anxious to have all the glory, he generously withdrew this claim, and advised them strongly to go on with the enterprise alone. This was definitely settled, Tone being appointed to accompany the expedition. Hoche explained privately to his Irish friends that he favoured the Dutch scheme mainly because it would rouse the French navy to action. Once the Dutch were in Ireland, he expected to follow in little less than a month.

Tone returned to Germany for his trunk, and Hoche, meeting him at Cologne, told him in highest delight that exactly what he expected had come about. The French Minister of Marine, urged by jealousy of the Dutch, was getting ready a fleet at Brest for the invasion of Ireland, and he was ordered to return to Brest and take command. Hoche's eagerness was sharpened by a desire to rival the achievements of Buonaparte, then rising to fame, of whom he was somewhat jealous and critical. The friends then parted—Hoche for Brest, Tone for the Hague, congratulating each other on the prospect of meeting and fighting side by side on the green sod of Ireland.

Alas! Alas! The hopes which now sprang up in the Irish exile's heart were doomed to disappointment even more bitter than that which had blighted his heart in Bantry Bay. Through the month of July the Dutch fleet was ready to embark, but was shut up in the Texel by adverse winds, whilst a British fleet, increasing in power day by day, held the North Sea. Some quotations from Tone's diary at this era will show the state of his mind:—

"July 27th, 28th. (On board Admiral de Winter's flagship Vryheid.) . . . Suspense is more terrible than danger. Loving, as I do to distraction, my wife and dearest babies, I wish to Heaven we were under way to meet the enemy, with whom we should be up in an hour. It is terrible to see the two fleets so near, and to find ourselves so helpless. The sea is just now as smooth as a mill pond. Ten times since I began this note I have lifted my eyes to look at the enemy. Well, it cannot be that this inaction will continue long. I am now aboard twenty days, and we have not had twenty minutes of a fair wind to carry us out. Well! well!

August 1st, 2nd.—Everything goes on here from bad to worse, and I am tormented and unhappy more than I can express, so that I hate even to make these memorandums. Well, it cannot be helped. On the 30th, in the morning early, the wind was fair, the signal given to prepare to get under way, and everything ready, when, at the very instant we were about to weigh anchor and put to sea, the wind chopped about and left us. Nothing can be imagined more tormenting. The admiral having some distrust of his pilots (for it seems that the pilots here are all Orangists) made signal to all the chiefs of the fleet to know if they thought it possible to get out with the wind which then blew (E.S.E.), but their answer was unanimous in the negative, so there was an end of the business. In an hour after the wind hauled round more to the S, and blew a gale, with thunder and lightning; so it was well we were not caught in the shoals which environ the entry of this abominable road. At last it fixed in the S.W., almost the very worst quarter possible, where it has remained steadily ever since. Not to lose time, the admiral sent out an officer with a letter addressed to Admiral Duncan, but in fact to reconnoitre the enemy's force. He returned yesterday with a report that Duncan's fleet is of seventeen sail of the line, including two or three three-deckers, which is pleasant. . . . Wind still S.W. Damn it! damn it! damn it! I am to-day twenty-five days aboard, and at a time when twenty-five hours are of importance. There seems to be a fate in this business. Five weeks, I believe six weeks, the English fleet was paralysed by the mutinies at Portsmouth, Plymouth, and the Nore. The sea was open, and nothing to prevent both the Dutch and French fleets to put to sea. Well, nothing was ready; that previous opportunity which we can never expect to return was lost, and now that at last we are ready here the wind is against us, the mutiny is quelled, and we are sure to be attacked by a superior force. At Brest it is, I fancy, still worse. Had we been in Ireland at the moment of the insurrection at the Nore, we should beyond a doubt, have had at least that fleet, and God only knows the influence which such an event might have had on the whole British navy. The destiny of Europe might have been changed for ever; but, as I have already said, that occasion is lost, and we must now do as well as we can. "*Le vin est tiré, il faut le boire!*"

On August 5th two Northern Unitedmen arrived at the Texel, and joined Wolfe Tone on board the Vryheid. These were Lowry, of County Down, and John Tennant, of Belfast. They informed him that the people of Ireland were greatly discouraged by the fact that the opportunity afforded by the mutiny at the Nore had not been availed of by France. MacNeven, they said, had left for France in July to appeal for immediate action, and Bartholomew Teeling had accompanied them as far as Hamburg. There they had seen a letter of Tone's to his sister, and had sent Teeling back to Ireland to inform the Unitedmen of the intended Dutch expedition, whilst they had made their way to the Texel hoping to take part in it. The remainder of the time which Tone spent with the Dutch fleet was brightened by the presence of these two friends. The wind continued foul as ever. Admiral Duncan's squadron was reinforced; hope faded in Tone's heart, and his diary became more and more despondent; but at least he had comrades now to sympathise with his impatience and despair. Projects for the invasion of the east coast of England and even of Scotland were put forward, but resulted in nothing. At length in the middle of August Lowry and Tennant departed *via* the Hague to Paris, and early in September Tone was despatched to Germany to confer with General Hoche as to what plan the Dutch and French armies could conjointly take.

More than a month after his departure the long-delayed encounter between the English and Dutch fleets came off. De Winter, after a gallant struggle, was utterly defeated, and Tone congratulated himself that he was not present during the engagement in these words: "It was well I was not on board the Vryheid. If I had it would have been a pretty piece of business. I fancy I am not to be caught at sea by the English; for this is the second escape I have had, and on land I mock at them!"

Alas! alas! within a year he was doomed to meet the English on the sea and fall into their hands as a prisoner.

Chapter XVII.

EXIT HOCHE—ENTER BUONAPARTE.

WE go back in history to the month of September, before the sea-fight at the Texel. Tone had been sent to Germany to interview Hoche, whose headquarters were at Wetzlar. He was alarmed and horrified to find the best friend of Ireland in the grasp of a fatal illness. His physician did not seem to understand the gravity of the case, and Hoche himself, though weak and ill, never dreamed of death, but spoke of the projected Irish campaign, and entered into the accounts of the Texel affair with the greatest interest. Tone alone amongst those who surrounded him seems to have realised that his end was near. On September 19th, in the morning, his worst fears were realised. The young general died of a rapid consumption, to the inconsolable grief of Tone, who, however, lost no time in returning to Paris. The governing power there had changed hands, and he was glad to find that Lewines had already established an understanding with the new Ministers, of whom the chief were Barras, Pleville le Peley (Minister of Marine), and Talleyrand Perigord (whom Tone had met before in Philadelphia), Minister for Foreign Affairs. But the man in whose hands the destiny of Ireland now lay was not any one of these heads of departments.

The security of France depended upon the strength of her army. The victorious campaign in Italy had proved to the menacing monarchies of Europe that the Republic was not only strong enough to maintain its rule within the borders of France, but to strike terror to the hearts of foes beyond her frontier. Now that Hoche was dead, the star of Buonaparte shone forth with unrivalled lustre. Tone saw the necessity of appealing to him to take up the Irish enterprise of Hoche, and on November 9th, 1797, wrote offering to serve under him.

The Ministers meantime assured Lewines and Tone that they would never abandon their design of humbling England, and one day, between the 18th and 21st of December, Tone at length found himself face to face with the Man of Destiny. His account of this historic occasion we must quote in full.

"December 18th-21st.—General Desaix brought Lewines and me this morning, and introduced us to Buonaparte at his house in the Rue Chantereine. He lives in the greatest simplicity; his house is small but neat, and all the furniture and ornaments in the most classical taste. He is about five feet six inches high, slender and well made, but stoops considerably. He looks at least ten years older than he is, owing to the great fatigues he underwent in his immortal campaign of Italy. His face is that of a profound thinker, but bears no marks of that great enthusiasm and unceasing activity by which he has been so much distinguished. It is rather to my mind the countenance of a mathematician than of a general. He has a fine eye, and a great firmness about his mouth; he speaks low and hollow. So much for his manner and figure. We had not much discourse with him, and what little there was, was between him and Lewines, to whom as our Ambassador I gave the *pas*. We told him that Tennant was about to depart for Ireland, and was ready to charge himself with his orders, if he had any to give. He desired us to bring him the same evening, and so we took our leave. In the evening we returned with Tennant, and Lewines had a good deal of conversation with him; that is to say, Lewines *insensed* him a good deal on Irish affairs, of which he appears a good deal uninformed. For example, he seems convinced that our population is not more than two millions, which is nonsense. Buonaparte listened, but said very little. When all this was finished he desired that Tennant should put off his departure a few days, and then turning to me, asked whether I was not an adjutant-general, to which I answered that I had the honour to be attached to General Hoche in that capacity. He then asked me where I had learned to speak French, to which I replied that I had learned the little I knew since my arrival in France about twenty months ago. He then desired us to return the next evening but one at the same hour, and so we parted. As to my French, I am ignorant whether it was the purity or the barbarism of my diction which drew his attention, and as I shall never inquire, it must remain as a historical doubt, to be investigated by the learned of future ages.

December 23rd—Called this evening on Buonaparte, by appointment, with Tennant and Lewines, and saw him for about five minutes. Lewines gave him a copy of the memorials I delivered to the Government in February, 1796 (nearly two years ago), and which, fortunately, have been well verified in every material fact by everything that has taken place in Ireland since. He also gave him Taylor's map, and showed him half a dozen of Hoche's letters, which Buonaparte read over. He then desired us to return in two or three days, with such documents as we were possessed of, and in the meantime that Tennant should postpone his departure. We then left him. His manner is cold, and he speaks very little; it is not, however, so dry as that of Hoche, but seems rather to proceed from languor than anything else. He is perfectly civil, however, to us, but from anything we have yet seen or heard from him, it is impossible to augur anything good or bad. We have now seen the greatest man in Europe three times, and I am astonished to think how little I have to record about him. I am sure I wrote ten times as much about my first interview with Charles de la Croix, but then I was a greenhorn; I am now a little used to see great men, and great statesmen and great generals, and that has in some degree broke down my admiration. Yet, after all, it is a droll thing that I should become acquainted with Buonaparte. This time twelve months I arrived in Brest from Bantry Bay. Well, the third time, they say, is the charm. My next chance, I hope, will be with the *Armée d'Angleterre—Allons! Vive la République.*"

With these interesting negotiation the year 1797 ended. Tone had now settled his family in Paris, his brother Matthew, who arrived in November from America, being of the number.

Chapter XVIII.

'NINETY-EIGHT.

NOW dawned the year of glory and terror, for Tone the year of death, eventful NINETY-EIGHT. Its first day found him in Paris among his dearest ones, and brought him letters and news from his father in Ireland, and his favourite brother far away in India. His first entry in his dairy was to wish himself "the compliments of the season, a Merry Christmas, and a Happy New Year." On his birthday in the following June, he made the last long entry in that famous journal. Up till that date we get glimpses of what was going on in Ireland, as the news reached him. Then the journal abruptly ceased; he was trying to send arms and men across the sea to sustain that desperate fight for freedom, and too busy to make the daily record. The story of his life told thus far by himself was completed in its last tragic heroic episodes by the pen of his son. We must not wander away from the life of Tone to give any detailed account of the events taking place in Ireland. Let us open the pages of his dairy, and read exactly what he heard, and try to realise the rage of impatience which possessed him. In the month of March, he was ordered to military headquarters at Rouen, and remained there, hoping that Buonaparte was about to do something for Ireland, and eagerly expecting orders to proceed to the coast. Just before his departure he heard of the arrest of Arthur O'Connor and Father Quigley, at Margate, and on reaching Rouen there came news of worse disaster from Ireland.

"March 26th.—I see in the English papers of March 17th, from Irish papers of the 13th, news of the most disastrous and afflicting kind, as well for me individually as for the country at large. The English Government has arrested the whole committee of United Irishmen for the province of Leinster, including almost every man I know and esteem in the city of Dublin. Amongst them are Emmet, Mac-Neven, Dr. Sweetman Bond, Jackson and his son; warrants are likewise issued for the arrestation of Lord Edward Fitzgerald, M'Cormick, and Sampson, who have not however yet been found. It is by far the most terrible blow which the cause of liberty in Ireland has yet sustained. I know not whether in the whole party it would be possible to replace the energy, talents, and integrity of which we are deprived by this most unfortunate of events. I have not received such a shock since I left Ireland. It is terrible to think of in every point of view. Government will move heaven and earth to destroy them. What a triumph at this moment for Fitzgibbon! These arrestations following so closely on that of O'Connor, give rise to very strong suspicions of treachery in my mind. I cannot bear to write or think longer on this dreadful event. Well, if our unfortunate country is doomed to sustain the unspeakable loss of so many brave and virtuous citizens, woe be to their tyrants if ever we reach our destination. I feel my mind growing every hour more savage. Measures appear to me now justified by necessity, which six months ago I would have regarded with horror. There is now no medium. Government has drawn the sword and will not recede but to superior force *if ever that force arrives.* But it does not signify threatening. Judge of my feelings as an individual when Emmet and Russell are in prison, and in imminent peril of a violent and ignominious death. What revenge can satisfy me for the loss of the two men I most esteemed on earth? Well once more, it does not signify threatening. If they are sacrificed, and I ever arrive, as I hope to do in Ireland, it will not go well with their enemies. This blow has completely deranged me—I can scarcely write connectedly."

(His distress and anxiety was increased by the fact that General Buonaparte, though presumably preparing an armament against England on the Channel coast, went off to a Mediterranean port, and finally embarked for Egypt. On April 25th William Hamilton, who afterwards shared in the conspiracy of Emmet and Russell, arrived a fugitive from London, and brought vague news of the breaking out of a rebellion in the South of Ireland. In the middle of May he went from Rouen to see his family in Paris, and whilst there heard news, which is thus recorded.)

"May 20th.—During my stay in Paris, I read in the English papers a long account from the *Dublin Journal* of a visitation held by the Chancellor in Trinity College, the result of which was the expulsion of nineteen students, and the suspension for three years of my friend Whitely Stokes."

(Robert Emmet was among the expelled students, and Moore, the poet, amongst those examined as to the existence of secret societies among the students. At the end of May, the English Fleet appeared before Havre, and proceeded to bombard it. Tone was ordered off there, and during the month of June commanded a battery in its defence. No determined attack was made, but he had some gunnery practice, and the thrilling experience of being actually under English fire. This occurrence took place on the day of Antrim fight, the 7th June.)

"I defy any man to know whether he is brave or not until he is tried, and I am very far from boasting of myself on that score; but the fact is, and I was right glad of it, that when I found myself at my battery, and saw the enemy bearing down upon us, and as I thought to begin the cannonade, though I cannot say with truth that I was perfectly easy, yet neither did I feel at all disconcerted, and I am satisfied as far as a man in that situation can judge of himself, that I should have done my duty well, and without any great effort of resolution. The crowd and the bustle, the noise, and especially the conviction that the eyes of the cannoniers were fixed on the *chapeau galonné*, settled me at once; it is the etiquette in such cases that the General stands conspicuous on the parapet, whilst the canoniers are covered by the *épaulement* which is truly amusing for him that commands. Nevertheless, I have no doubt that it is easier to behave well on the parapet exposed to all the fire, than in the battery, where the danger is much less. I had time to make all these, and divers otherwise remarks during my stay, for it was six in the evening before the English stood off, and on the faith of an honest man, I cannot truly say I was sorry when I saw them decidedly turn their backs.

"June 9th to 12th.—Yesterday I read in the French papers an account of the acquittal of Arthur O'Connor, at Maidstone, and of his being taken instantly into custody again. Undoubtedly, Pitt means to send him to Ireland, in hopes of finding a more complaisant jury. Quigley, the Priest, is found guilty; it seems he has behaved admirably well. . . . My satisfaction at this triumph of O'Connor is almost totally destroyed by a second article in this same paper, which mentions that Lord Edward Fitzgerald has been arrested in Thomas Street, Dublin, after a most desperate resistance, in which himself, the magistrate, one Swann and Captain Ryan who commanded the guard were severly wounded. I cannot describe the effect which this intelligence had on me, it brought on a spasm in my stomach, which confined me all day. I knew Fitzgerald but very little, but I honour and venerate his character, which he has uniformly sustained, and in this last instance illustrated. What miserable wretches by his side are the gentry of Ireland! I would rather be Fitzgerald as he is now, wounded in his dungeon, than Pitt at the head of the British Empire. What a noble fellow! Of the first family in Ireland, with an easy fortune, a beautiful wife, and family of lovely children, the certainty of a splendid appointment under government if he would condescend to support their measures. He has devoted himself wholly to the emancipation of *his* country and sacrificed everything to it, even his blood. My only consolation is the hope that his enemies have no capital charge against him, and will be obliged to limit their rage to his imprisonment. The city and county of Dublin are proclaimed under martial law. When they combine this with the late seizure of cannon at Clarke's, I am strongly inclined to think that Fitzgerald was meditating an attack on the capital! Poor fellow! He is not the first Fitzgerald who has sacrificed himself to the cause of his country. There is a wonderful similarity of principle and fortune between him and his ancestor Lord Thomas, in the reign of Henry VII., who lost his head on Tower Hill for a gallant, but fruitless attempt, to recover the independence of Ireland. God send the catastrophe of his noble descendant be not the same. I dread everything for him, and my only consolation is in the speculation of revenge. If the blood of this brave young man be shed by the hand of his enemies, it is no ordinary vengeance, which will content the people, whenever the day of retribution arrives. I cannot express the rage I feel at my own helplessness at this moment, but what can I do? Let me if possible think no more, it sets me half mad.

"June 13th.—This morning at eight o'clock, I was

roused by two or three guns. I dressed myself in a hurry and ran to the batteries, where I arrived before the cannoniers, or any of my comrades. . . . We fired two or three shots from the battery merely to show the gunboats that we were there to support them, but without any expectation of reaching the enemy, who all this time never condescended to return us one gun. After about half-an-hour the fire ceased, and the enemy stood off. I do not well conceive the object of these two visits last night and this morning. It is now 11 a.m., and we expect them again with the evening tide, maybe then, we shall see something. I have been running over in my mind the list of my friends, and of the men whom, without being so intimately connected with them, I most esteem. Scarcely do I find one who is not or has not been in exile or prison, and in jeopardy of his life. To begin with, Russell and Emmet, the two dearest of my friends at this moment are in prison on a capital charge. MacNeven and J. Sweetman, my old fellow-labourers in the Catholic cause; Edward Fitzgerald, Arthur and Roger O'Connor, whom though I know less personally, I do not less esteem; Sampson, Bond, Jackson, and his son, still in prison; Robert and William Simms, the men in the world to whose friendship I am most obliged, but just discharged. Neilson, Haslett, and M'Cracken, the same M'Cormick absconded; Rowan and Dr. Reynolds, in America; Lewines, Tennant, Lowry, Hamilton, Teeling, Tandy, and others with whom I have little or no acquaintance, but whom I must presume to be victims of their patriotism, not to speak of my own family in France, Germany, and elsewhere. Stokes disgraced on suspicion of virtue. It is a gloomy catalogue for a man to cast his eyes over. Of all my political connections I see but John Keogh who has escaped, and how he has had that good fortune is to me a miracle.

"June 17th-18th.—The news I have received this

morning, partly by the papers and partly by letters from my wife and brother, are of the last importance. As suspected, the brave and unfortunate Fitzgerald was meditating an attack on the capital, which was to have taken place a few days after that on which he was arrested. He is since dead in prison; his career is finished, gloriously for himself, and whatever be the event, his memory will live for ever in the heart of every honest Irishman. He was a gallant fellow. For us who remain as yet, and may perhaps soon follow him, the only way to lament his death is to endeavour to revenge it. Among his papers, it seems, was found the plan of the insurrection, the proclamation intended to be published and several others by which those of the leaders of the people who have thus far escaped have been implicated, and several of them seized. Among others I see Tom Braughall, Lawless, son of Lord Cloncurry, Curran, son of the barrister; Chambers and P. Byrne, printers, with several others whom I cannot recollect. All this, including the death of the brave Fitzgerald, has, it appears, but accelerated matters. The insurrection has formally commenced in several counties of Leinster, especially Kildare and Wexford. The details in the French papers are very imperfect, but I see there have been several actions—Monastereven, Naas, Clane, and Prosperous, the three last immediately in my ancient neighbourhood. There have been skirmishes, generally, as is at first to be expected, to the advantage of the army. At Prosperous the Cork Militia were surprised and defeated. The villains —to bear arms against their country! Kilcullen is burnt. at Carlow four hundred Irish, it is said, were killed, at Castledermot fifty. In return, in County Wexford, where appears to be their principal force, they have defeated a party of six hundred English, killed three hundred and the commander, Colonel Walpole, and taken five pieces of cannon. This victory, small as it is, will give the people courage, and show them that a red coat is no more invincible than a grey one. At Rathmines there has been an affair of cavalry, where the Irish had the worst, and two of their leaders named Ledwich and Keogh taken, and, I presume, immediately executed. I much fear that the last is Cornelius, eldest son to my friend John Keogh, and a gallant lad; if it be so, I shall regret him sincerely. But how many other valuable lives must be sacrificed before the fortune of Ireland be decided! Dr. Esmonde and eight other gentlemen of my county have been hanged; at Nenagh the English whip the most respectable inhabitants till their blood flows into the kennel. The atrocious barbarity of their conduct is only to be excelled by the folly of it; never yet was a rebellion, as they call it, quenched by such means. The eighteen thousand victims sacrificed by Alva in the Low Countries in five years and on the scaffold did not prevent the establishment of liberty in Holland. From the blood of every one of the martyrs of the liberty of Ireland will spring, I hope, thousands to revenge their fall. . . . What will the French Government do in the present crisis? After all, their aid appears to be indispensable; for the Irish have no means but numbers and courage—powerful and indispensable instruments it is true, but which, after all, require arms and ammunition, and I fear they are but poorly provided with either. If the Irish can hold out till winter I have every reason to hope that the French will assist them effectually. All I dread is that they may be overpowered before that time. What a state my mind is in at this moment. In all this business I do not see one syllable about the North, which astonishes me more than I can express. Are they afraid? Have they changed their opinions? What can be the cause of their passive submission at this moment, so little suited to their former energy and zeal? I remember what Digges said to Russell and me five or six years ago: " If ever the South is roused, I would rather have one Southern than twenty Northerns.' Digges was a man of great sense and observation. He was an American, and had no local or provincial prejudices. Was he right in his opinion? A very little time will let us see. If it should prove so, what a mortification to me, who have so long looked up with admiration to the North, and especially to Belfast! It cannot be that they have changed their principles; it must be that circumstances render all exertions on their part as yet impossible."

Chapter XIX.

COMING BACK TO IRELAND.

WITH that long record on his last birthday and a hasty note to the effect that he was recalled to Paris to consult with the Ministry, Wolfe Tone's diary ends. His son, writing the concluding chapters of his life's story, was well qualified to give an account of the dealings of France with Ireland at that fateful crisis. This son grew to manhood's years in France, and served in the army of Napoleon. Though devoted personally to that great man, he acknowledges with regret that Napoleon's indifference was the cause of Ireland's defeat; that whereas Hoche and Carnot were true friends of Ireland and Republicans in principle, Napoleon was thinking only of glory. "When Carnot," he writes, "the only able and honest man in the Councils of the Directory, was proscribed, and when General Hoche died, the friends of a revolution in that island lost every chance of assistance from France. Those two great statesmen and warriors, earnest in the cause of which they perceived the full importance to the interests of their country and to the extension of Republican principles, had planned the expeditions of Bantry Bay and of the Texel on the largest and most effective scale which the naval resources of France and of Holland could afford." Of Buonaparte he says, "It is with extreme reluctance that I feel myself called upon by the nature of my subject to point out any errors in the conduct of the sovereign, chief, and benefactor under whom I bore my first arms and received my first wounds, of him who decorated me with the insignia of the Legion of Honour, and whom I served with constant fidelity and devotion to the last moments of his reign. But the imperious voice of truth compels me to attribute to the influences and prejudices of General Buonaparte, at that period, the prime cause of the failure of the third expedition for the liberation of Ireland. . . To the enterprise against Ireland, the favourite object of Hoche, and to prosecute which he was ostensibly recalled, he felt a secret but strong repugnance. Though the liberation of that country might prostrate for ever the power of England and raise the Republic to the pinnacle of fortune, it offered him no prospects of aggrandisement. . . When my father was presented to him and attached to his army as adjutant-general, he received him with cold civility, but entered into no communications. His plans were already formed. Ostensibly a great force was organised on the Western coasts of France, under the name of the army of England; but the flower of the troops were successively withdrawn and marched to the Mediterranean; the eyes of Europe were fixed on these operations, but from their eccentricity their object could not be discovered. My father, despatched, as may be seen in his journals, to headquarters at Rouen, and employed in unimportant movements on the coast, in the bombardment of Havre, etc., heard with successive pangs of disappointment that Buonaparte had left Paris for the south; that he had arrived at Toulon; that he had embarked and sailed with a powerful expedition in the beginning of June."

It was not till July we have seen that Tone was recalled to Paris to take council with the Ministers of War and Marine. The insurrection was then virtually over, but fugitives arriving from Ireland were of opinion that on the appearance of foreign aid the people would again fly to arms. It was then arranged to despatch small detachments to various ports to keep alive the insurrection till the arrival of the main force of invasion. For this purpose General Humbert was quartered at Rochelle with 1,000 men, Hardi with 3,000 at Brest, and General Kilmaine (an Irishman by birth) held 9,000 in reserve.

General Humbert, waxing impatient of delay, on hearing the news from Irish refugees, sailed without orders from the port of Rochelle. The history of this daring enterprise is well known. Landing in Killala Bay, he rallied the peasantry of Connaught, sent the British racing at Castlebar, and was finally defeated at Ballinamuck. There were three Irishmen with his party, Bartholomew Teeling, Sullivan, nephew of Madgett, and Matthew, brother of Wolfe Tone. Teeling and Tone were executed in Dublin; Sullivan, being taken for a Frenchman, escaped that fate.

The news of Humbert's arrival and first successes made the French Directory conclude to despatch the second expedition from Brest, under General Hardi. It was not, however, till September 20th they were ready to sail. Commodore Bompard commanded the little fleet, which consisted of one sail of the line (the Hoche) and eight frigates.

Previous to the departure of this squadron Napper Tandy and a number of the United Irish refugees sailed ahead in a fast frigate (the Anacreon), and reaching the coast of Donegal, spread a number of proclamations. Then hearing of Humbert's defeat through the postman of Rutland Island, whose mail-bags they seized, they put out to sea and arrived safely in Norway. Arriving at Hamburg, Tandy and two friends, W. Corbett and Blackwell, were given into the hands of the English, and suffered years of imprisonment.

In departing on this desperate enterprise Tone had little hope of success. He had by this time become inured to disappointment. He was prepared to face the very worst, and the fact that his name was published in the French papers as being on board the Hoche betrayed him to his foes. He was in reality attached to General Kilmaine's force, which was to have gone last of all; but his dauntless heart could brook no further delay. Thousands had died that year for Ireland on battlefield and scaffold— old men and young, brave women and boys. Now, he, the leader, the organiser, who had breathed into the land the spirit of defiant insurrection, bade a calm but sad farewell to wife and little ones, and came sailing over the sea to take his place in the post of danger and win the deathless glory of the martyr's crown.

Chapter XX.

BATTLE, DEFEAT, AND FETTERS.

IT was to the coast of Ulster that the flagship bearing Wolfe Tone directed its way. He had all along looked upon that province as best prepared for war, and as the rising had been of short duration in Antrim and Down, he doubtless assumed that he would find the Northern United battalions less shattered than those of the western province. Humbert was still supposed to be waging war in North Connaught, so this flotilla came coastward to the most westerly county of Ulster, and into Lough

Swilly, the safest harbour of Donegal. We have good reason to believe that this county was to some extent organised to receive them. As long ago as the winter of '96, when a French invasion was expected, the people of Northwest Donegal were up in arms, and a state of insurrection prevailed. The Rev. Thomas Hamilton, rector of Clonavaddock, was obliged to call in the military from Derry, and has left an interesting account of the disturbances. That these Donegal insurgents were made aware of the Bantry Bay expedition is highly probable. We received in fact a remarkable confirmation of this theory lately, when Mr. Frank Hugh O'Donnell informed us that his great grandfather died of exposure and starvation on the hills above Dunfanaghy in the winter of 1796. Mr. O'Donnell was not aware that there was any recorded rising at that time, but had always heard that his ancestor had returned from the continent with a view to rousing Tir-conal, and drilling the peasantry. Possibly this ancestor was the moving spirit in that Clonavaddock rising. He would hardly have died upon the hill-sides had not the soldiery been in pursuit.

Lough Swilly, into which the flagship Hoche and the fleet of frigates came on that October day, 1798, is not only one of the most beautiful bays in Ireland, but one of the most remarkable in history. On a hill looking over its waters stands the ruined wall of Aileach, the royal palace of the north, on the Lough shore stands the priory of Rathmullan, where Hugh O'Neill and the fugitive chiefs of Tirconal spent their last night in Ireland. Over Lough Swilly's waves went the ship of doom that bore them to death in exile; and here too, nearly a generation earlier, anchored the ship of Wines, which John Perrot sent to capture Hugh Roe O'Donnell. The peasantry who crowded upon cliff and hill to watch these warships come in, must have whispered one to another old prophecies and rumours regarding the downfall of the Sassenach, sayings of Columcille the prophet, that from this land the deliverance of Ireland was to come.

The ships had hardly made their way between the promontories of Fannet and Dunaff when those which were last suddenly changed their course, and signals of alarm were exchanged. The breaking dawnlight shone upon the sails of a pursuing squadron. Bompard, the admiral, signalled from the Hoche to the lighter vessels to fly from the bay, and soon they were tacking away seaward; but the Hoche, too large a vessel to make way in a light wind, was prepared for action. A boat was launched from one of the schooners ere it fled, and the men coming alongside asked for the admiral's last orders. Bompard turned to Wolfe Tone, who was busy preparing the men of one battery for action. "Our contest is hopeless," he said, "we fight only for the honour of the flag. We will fall in action or be made prisoners of war. What will become of you?" The officers one and all crowded round their Irish comrade, and urged him to go. He looked after the white sails scudding across the sea; then at the towering British warships coming nearer, nearer, and sending now and then a white cloud of smoke across the water, whilst the boom, boom of the cannon echoed from Dunree to Knockalla and back again. The sailors stepped to the ship's side and urged haste.

"Shall it be said that I fled whilst the French were fighting the battles of my country?" Thus came his answer calm and determined. The Frenchmen knew further entreaty was useless, so away went the boat, and soon the Hoche was making her way out of Lough Swilly, whilst Tone stood up in his battery and turned his face to the foe.

The ship on which he stood bore the name of Hoche, the great dead general, Ireland's truest friend, and worthy of Hoche's name she proved herself that day. Four British men of war and a frigate bore down on her, and for six hours she sustained a desperate, hopeless fight. Her masts and rigging were swept away, her scuppers flowed with blood, her wounded filled the cockpit, her shattered ribs yawned at each new stroke and let in five feet of water in the hold, her rudder was carried off, and she floated a dismantled wreck upon the waters. For six long hours Tone rallied his gunners, and directed their fire, exposing himself recklessly to the balls from the British cannon. He courted death, well knowing the doom which awaited him should he fall into the hands of the foemen.

At last the ship struck, and the remaining crew were brought prisoners on board the enemy's deck. Tradition says that Tone flung his sword into the sea rather than surrender it to the enemy. Some days later he was brought a prisoner to Letterkenny, still unrecognised, and treated as a Frenchman, till a former college acquaintance, Sir George Hill, meeting him at breakfast, greeted him by name. He was instantly seized and fettered. As the chains were fastened around him, chafing at the indignity shown to the army of France, he would have flung his uniform from him, but restraining himself, he calmly stretched forth his arms, and said, "For the cause which I have embraced I feel prouder to wear these chains than if I were decorated with the star and garter of England."

His first night as a prisoner was spent in a cell in the old gaol in Derry Diamond. Thence he wrote to Lord Cavan, who had gone to Buncrana, presumably to attend to the transporting of other prisoners.

From Derry he was brought riding southward to Dublin, and on the journey fascinated and astonished his attendant guards by his dauntless spirits and even gaiety.

So after those years of exile Wolfe Tone came back to the city of his birth. He thought of brave Fitzgerald and how a few short months ago he had pitied his hapless fate. Now death was coming near to him and his beloved wife and helpless little ones were to be left in a position as pitiable as Pamela and her children. He was imprisoned in the barracks prison, and his trial was to be by court-martial. Facing his soldier judges he scorned to defend or exculpate himself. He acknowledged that he had taken up arms to free Ireland; but as a French officer he asked a soldier's death. This last request was denied, and the judges, gloating over their victim's evident repugnance, sentenced him to the gallows. Proudly and calmly Tone heard his sentence, and was led back to his cell.

Chapter XXI.

THE COURT-MARTIAL.

WE quote in full the account given of this memorable triumph from Tone's life by his son, and, in addition, we would say that his behaviour on this trying occasion won for him the admiration and respect of the general public. The Duke of Argyle's recent attempt to represent him as a scamp who took to politics out of a mere love of adventure, is best confuted by reference to the journals of to-day. He is alluded to in a Dublin journal dedicated to Lord Clare, his arch-enemy, as "that highly talented and unfortunate gentleman, Theobald Wolfe Tone, Esquire." Men in Parliament, and even in power, spoke of him with pity and respect, recognising him, as they could not fail to do, as a man of remarkable ability. Sir John Moore, the soldier hero of Corunna, was amongst those present at the trial, who has recorded his impression of Tone's conduct on the occasion. William Tone's account proceeds as follows:—

Though the reign of terror was drawing to a close, and

Lord Cornwallis had restored some appearance of legal order and regular administration in the kingdom, a prisoner of such importance to the Irish Protestant ascendancy party, as the founder and leader of the United Irish Society, and the most formidable of their adversaries, was not to be trusted to the delays and common forms of law. Though the Court of King's Bench was then sitting, preparations were instantly made for trying him summarily before a court-martial. But before I give an account of this trial, and of the nature of his defence, it will be necessary to remove some erroneous impressions on these subjects which I have seen stated, both in Curran's Life, by his son, and in the very fair and liberal comments of the *London New Monthly Magazine*. A prevailing notion in both these works is, that from my father's early dislike to legal studies, and inaccurate acquaintance with the English laws, he considered his French commission as a protection, and pleaded it in his defence. It is impossible to read his speech on the trial, and preserve this idea. Though he used to laugh at his little proficiency in legal lore, he knew perfectly well that the course he had deliberately taken subjected him to the utmost severity of the British laws. Nor was he ignorant that, by the custom of the land, and the very tenor of those laws, his trial, as it was conducted, was informal. He never was legally condemned; for, though a subject of the Crown (not of Britain, but of Ireland), he was not a military man in that kingdom; he had taken no military oath, and of course the court-martial which tried him had no power to pronounce on his case, which belonged to the regular criminal tribunals. But his heart was sunk in despair at the total failure of his hopes, and he did not wish to survive them. To die with honour was his only wish, and his only request to be shot like a soldier. For this purpose he preferred himself to be tried by a court-martial, and proffered his French commission, not to defend his life, but as a proof of his rank, as he stated himself on his trial.

If further proof were required that my father was perfectly aware of his fate, according to the English law, his own Journals, written during the Bantry Bay expedition, afford an incontestable one. (See Journal of December 26, 1796.) "If we are taken, my fate will not be a mild one; the best I can expect is to be shot as an *emigré réntré*, unless I have the good fortune to be killed in the action; for most assuredly, if the enemy will have us, he must fight for us. Perhaps I may be reserved for a trial, for the sake of striking terror into others, in which case I shall be hanged as a traitor, and embowelled, etc. As to the embowelling, '*Je m'en fiche.*' If ever they hang me, they are welcome to embowel me if they please. These are pleasant prospects! Nothing on earth could sustain me now but the consciousness that I am engaged in a just and righteous cause."

But my father also knew that political considerations will often supersede the letter of the laws. The only chance on which he had formerly relied was, that the French Government would interfere, and claim him with all its power and credit; to that, and to threats of severe retaliation, he knew that the British Cabinet would yield, as they did about a year afterwards in the case of Napper Tandy. A curious fact, and which is not generally known, perhaps, even to that gallant soldier himself, is, that Sir Sidney Smith was detained by Carnot in the Temple for that very purpose, like a prisoner of state, rather than a prisoner of war.

The time of my father's trial was deferred a few days, by the officers appointed to sit on the court-martial receiving marching orders. At length, on Saturday, November 10, 1798, a new court was assembled, consisting of General Loftus, who performed the functions of President, Colonels Vandeleur, Daly, and Wolfe, Major Armstrong, and a Captain Curran; Mr. Patterson performed the functions of Judge Advocate.

At an early hour the neighbourhood of the barracks was crowded with eager and anxious spectators. As soon as the doors were thrown open, they rushed in and filled every corner of the hall.

Tone appeared in the uniform of a Chef de Brigade (Colonel). The firmness and cool serenity of his whole deportment gave to the awe-struck assembly the measure of his soul. Nor could his bitterest enemies, whatever they deemed of his political principles, and of the necessity of striking a great example, deny him the praise of determination and magnanimity.

The members of the Court having taken the usual oath, the Judge Advocate proceeded to inform the prisoner that the court-martial before which he stood was appointed, by the Lord Lieutenant of the Kingdom, to try whether he had or had not acted traitorously and hostilely against his Majesty, to whom, as a natural born subject, he owed all allegiance, from the very fact of his birth in that kingdom. And, according to the usual form, he called upon him to plead guilty or not guilty.

Tone. "I mean not to give the Court any useless trouble, and wish to spare them the idle task of examining witnesses. I admit all the facts alleged, and only request leave to read an address, which I have prepared for this occasion."

Col. Daly. "I must warn the prisoner, that, in acknowledging those *facts*, he admits to his prejudice that he has acted *traitorously* against his Majesty. Is such his intention?"

Tone. "Stripping this charge of the technicality of its terms, it means, I presume, by the word 'traitorously,' that I have been found in arms against the soldiers of the King, in my native country. I admit this accusation in its most extended sense, and request again to explain to the Court the reasons and motives of my conduct."

The Court then observed that they would hear his address, provided he confined himself within the bounds of moderation He rose, and began in these words.—

"Mr. President, and Gentlemen of the Court-Martial,— I mean not to give you the trouble of bringing judicial proof to convict me, legally, of having acted in hostility to the Government of his Britannic Majesty in Ireland. I admit the fact. From my earliest youth I have regarded the connection between Ireland and Great Britain as the curse of the Irish nation, and felt convinced that, whilst it lasted, this country could never be free nor happy. My mind has been confirmed in this opinion by the experience of every succeeding year, and the conclusions which I have drawn from every fact before my eyes. In consequence, I determined to apply all the powers, which my individual efforts could move, in order to separate the two countries.

"That Ireland was not able, of herself, to throw off the yoke, I knew. I therefore sought for aid wherever it was to be found. In honourable poverty I rejected offers, which, to a man in my circumstances, might be considered highly advantageous. I remained faithful to what I thought the cause of my country, and sought in the French Republic an ally to rescue three millions of my countrymen from"...

The President here interrupted the prisoner, observing that this language was neither relevant to the charge, nor such as ought to be delivered in a public court. One member said it seemed calculated only to inflame the minds of a certain description of people (the United Irishmen), many of whom might probably be present, and that therefore the Court ought not to suffer it. The Judge Advocate said he thought that if Mr. Tone meant this paper to be laid before his Excellency, in way of *extenuation*, it must have a quite contrary effect if any of the foregoing part was suffered to remain.

Tone. "I shall urge this topic no further since it seems disagreeable to the Court, but shall proceed to read the few words which remain."

Gen. Loftus. "If the remainder of your address, Mr. Tone, is of the same complexion with what you have already read, will you not hesitate a moment in proceeding, since you have learned the opinion of the Court?"

Tone. "I believe there is nothing in what remains for me to say which can give any offence. I mean to express my feelings and gratitude towards the Catholic body in whose cause I was engaged."

Gen. Loftus. "That seems to have nothing to say to the charge against you, to which only you are to speak. If you have anything to offer in defence or extenuation of that charge the Court will hear you; but they beg that you will confine yourself to that subject."

Tone. "I shall, then, confine myself to some points relative to my connection with the French army. Attached to no party in the French Republic, without interest, without money, without intrigue, the openness and integrity of my views raised me to a high and confidential rank in its armies. I obtained the confidence of the Executive Directory, the approbation of my Generals, and I venture to add the esteem and affection of my brave comrades. When I review these circumstances I feel a secret and internal consolation which no reverse of fortune, no sentence in the power of this Court to inflict, can ever deprive me of, or weaken in any degree. Under the flag of the French Republic I originally engaged with a view to save and liberate my own country. For that purpose I have encountered the chances of war amongst strangers: for that purpose I have repeatedly braved the terrors of the ocean, covered, as I knew it to be, with the triumphant fleets of that Power which it was my glory and my duty to oppose. I have sacrificed all my views in life; I have courted poverty; I have left a beloved wife unprotected, and children whom I adored, fatherless. After such sacrifices in a cause which I have always conscientiously considered as the cause of justice and freedom—it is no great effort, as this day, to add, 'the sacrifice of my life.'

"But I hear it said that this unfortunate country has been a prey to all sorts of horrors. I sincerely lament it. I beg, however, it may be remembered that I have been absent four years from Ireland. To me these sufferings never can be attributed. I designed, by fair and open war, to procure the separation of the two countries. For open war I was prepared; but if, instead of that, a system of private assassination has taken place, I repeat, whilst I deplore it, that it is not chargeable on me. Atrocities, it seems, have been committed on both sides. I do not less deplore them. I detest them from my heart; and to those who know my character and sentiments, I may safely appeal for the truth of this assertion. With them I need no justification.

"In a cause like this success is everything. Success in the eyes of the vulgar fixes its merits. Washington succeeded and Kosciusko failed.

"After a combat nobly sustained, a combat which would have excited the respect and sympathy of a generous enemy, my fate was to become a prisoner. To the eternal disgrace of those who gave the order, I was brought hither in irons like a felon. I mention this for the sake of others; for me I am indifferent to it; I am aware of the fate which awaits me, and scorn equally the tone of complaint and that of supplication.

"As to the connection between this country and Great Britain, I repeat it, all that has been imputed to me—words, writings, and actions—I here deliberately avow. I have spoken and acted with reflection and on principle, and am ready to meet the consequences. Whatever be the sentence of this Court I am prepared for it. Its members will surely discharge their duty; I shall take care not to be wanting in mine."

This speech was pronounced in a tone so magnanimous,

so full of a noble and calm serenity as seemed deeply and visibly to affect all its hearers, the members of the Court not excepted. A pause ensued of some continuance, and silence reigned in the hall till interrupted by Tone himself, who inquired whether it was not usual to assign an interval between the sentence and execution? The Judge Advocate answered that the voices of the Court would be collected without delay, and the result transmitted forthwith to the Lord Lieutenant. If the prisoner therefore had any further observations to make, now was the moment.

Tone. "I wish to offer a few words relative to one single point—to the mode of punishment. In France, our *Emigrés*, who stand nearly in the same situation in which I suppose I now stand before you, are condemned to be shot. I ask that the Court should adjudge me the death of a soldier, and let me be shot by a platoon of grenadiers. I request this indulgence, rather in consideration of the uniform which I wear, the uniform of a Chef de Brigade in the French army, than from any personal regard to myself. In order to evince my claim to this favour, I beg that the Court may take the trouble to peruse my commission and letters of service in the French army. It will appear from these papers that I have not received them as a mask to cover me, but that I have been long and *bonâ fide* an officer in the French service."

Judge Advocate. "You must feel that the papers you allude to will serve as undeniable proofs against you."

Tone. "Oh!—*I know it well*—I have already admitted the facts, and I now admit the papers as full proofs of conviction."

The papers were then examined: they consisted of a brevet of Chef de Brigade from the Directory, signed by the Minister of War, of a letter of service, granting to him the rank of Adjutant-General, and of a passport.

General Loftus. "In those papers you are designated as serving in the army of England."

Tone. "I did serve in that army when it was commanded by Buonaparte, by Desaix, and by Kilmaine, who is, as I am, an Irishman, but I have also served elsewhere." Requested if he had anything further to observe, he said that nothing more occurred to him, except that the sooner his Excellency's approbation of their sentence was obtained the better. He would consider it as a favour if it could be obtained in an hour.

General Loftus then observed that the Court would undoubtedly submit to the Lord Lieutenant the address which he had read to them, and also the subject of his last demand. In transmitting the address, he, however, took care to efface all that part of it which he would not allow to be read, and which contained the dying speech and last words of the first apostle of Irish union and martyr of Irish liberty to his countrymen. Lord Cornwallis refused the last demand of my father, and he was sentenced to die the death of a traitor in forty-eight hours, on the 12th of November. This cruelty he had foreseen; for England, from the days of Llewellyn of Wales, and Wallace of Scotland, to those of Tone and Napoleon, has never shown mercy or generosity to a fallen enemy. He then, in perfect coolness and self-possession, determined to execute his purpose, and anticipate their sentence.

Chapter XXII.

DEATH IN PRISON.

THIS scene was enacted on November 10th, a Saturday. The execution was fixed for Monday, possibly because the trial was concluded at too late an hour to admit of the sentence being carried out the same day as in the case of Henry Joy M'Cracken, or perhaps because there was no scaffold ready. He was given, in any case, one day to spend in preparation for the next world, and to write his farewells to those he left behind.

Friends there were, who did not even yet despair of saving him. There were British prisoners (like Henry Sidney Smith) in the hands of France, and if time could be gained to admit of an appeal being made to the Republic, it was seen that they could have been held as sureties for the life of Tone. Curran, the great orator, whose voice had been ere this heard on behalf of many of the *United Men*, exerted himself to secure a postponement. He saw that the trial by court-martial was irregular when his Majesty's Court of King's Bench was sitting, and on Monday morning he presented himself before Lord Kilwarden, accompanied by Peter Tone, the patriot's aged father, and was actually successful in securing a warrant from that just and humane Judge, demanding that Tone should be brought before him to be tried again. The Military Judges were reluctant to give up their prey, and seemed determined to have him executed in defiance of the law.

Kilwarden despatched the Sheriff to the barracks to take the Provost Marshall and Major Sandys into custody and to bring Tone up for trial. In the interval of waiting, Lord Kilwarden displayed the utmost agitation and concern, and was moved, as Tone's son informs us, by feelings of pity and respect for the prisoner, whom he knew personally and whom he had shielded, as we have seen on another occasion, of danger. The Sheriff, at length, returned with news that produced a fearful sensation. The prisoner could not be brought there, nor yet executed, as he was lying at the point of death from a wound inflicted by his own hand.

Let us turn now from the court to the patriot's cell, and recount how he spent the last hours of his life.

He had absolutely refused to see any of his kindred or friends, and wrote on the evening after his trial to his father a respectful and affectionate letter, telling him his determination in this respect. He knew that his brave but susceptible heart would be melted by the pain of such a parting, and in the presence of his gaolers he dared not allow himself to be so shaken by grief. His wife's brothers and sister sent him friendly messages, but refusing to see anyone, he devoted his time that evening to writing an appeal to the French Directory and to General Kilmaine and Colonel Shee on behalf of his family. He then wrote to his wife a courageous, touching letter of farewell.

Provost Prison, Dublin Barracks,
Le 20, Brumaire an 7 (10th Nov., 1798).

"DEAREST LOVE—The hour is at last come when we must part. As no words can express what I feel for you and our children, I shall not attempt it; complaint of any kind would be beneath your courage and mine; be assured that I will die as I have lived, and that you will have no cause to blush for me. I have written on your behalf to the French Government, to the Minister of Marine, to General Kilmaine, and Mr. Shee. With the latter I wish you especially to advise. In Ireland I have written to your brother Harry, and to those of my friends who are about to go into exile, and who, I am sure, will not abandon you.

Adieu, dearest love; I find it impossible to finish this letter. Give my love to Mary; and, above all things, remember that you are now the only parent of our dearest children, and that the best proof you can give of your affection for me will be to preserve yourself for their education. God Almighty bless you all.

"Yours ever,
T. W. TONE."

"P.S.—I think you have found a friend in Wilson, who will not desert you."

Next day (Sunday) when the city resounded to the solemn notes of church bells another sound broke the stillness of the condemned cell. It was the knock, knock, knock of the hammers fixing together the timbers of his scaffold. He was, most likely, not aware that his friends, Peter Burrowes and Curran, were even then working hard to postpone the execution and save his life. He saw himself led to the very verge of the precipice. Rough hands were making ready to hurl him over and to exult over his strangled corpse. They had refused him a soldier's death and sentenced him to this. In haughty resentment he determined to take the last step himself. In this spirit of resolution he spent his last evening upon earth and penned one more letter to his dear wife, whose helpless fate alone caused him anxiety.

"DEAREST LOVE—I write just one letter to acquaint you that I have received assurances from your brother Edward of his determination to render every assistance and protection in his power; for which I have written to thank him most sincerely. Your sister has likewise sent me assurances of the same nature, and expressed a desire to see me, which I have refused, having determined to speak to no one of my friends, not even my father, from motives of humanity to them and myself. It is a very great consolation to me that your family are determined to support you; as to the manner of that assistance, I leave it to their affection for you, and your own excellent good sense to settle what manner will be most respectable for both parties.

"Adieu, dearest love. Keep your courage as I have kept mine; my mind is as tranquil at this moment as at any period of my life. Cherish my memory; and especially preserve your health and spirits for the sake of our dearest children.

"Your ever affectionate,
"T. WOLFE TONE.
"11th November, 1798."

It was at four o'clock in the morning that the prisoner's wounded condition was discovered by the sentry. To the surgeon who was summoned to attend him he found voice to say in the most collected manner—" I am sorry I have been so bad an anatomist." His wounds were bandaged, and for seven days and nights he lay in mortal agony. In escaping death on the gallows he had but condemned himself to that period of slow torture. His son has described, in words of unsurpassable pathos, that lengthened martyrdom. " Stretched on his bloody pallet in a dungeon, the first apostle of Irish Union, and most illustrious martyr of Irish Independence, counted each lingering hour during the last seven days and nights of his slow and silent agony. No one was allowed to approach him. Far from his adored family, and from all those friends whom he loved so dearly, the only forms which flitted before his eyes were those of the grim jailer and rough attendants of the prison; the only sounds which fell on his dying ear, the heavy tread of the sentry. He retained, however, the calmness of his soul and the possession of his faculties to the last And the consciousness of dying for his country, and in the cause of justice and liberty, illumined like a bright halo, his latest moments, and kept up his fortitude to the end. There is no situation under which those feelings will not support the soul of a patriot."

On the morning of the 19th of November he was seized with the spasms of approaching death. It is said that the surgeon who attended whispered that if he attempted to move or speak he must expire instantly, that he overheard him, and, making a slight movement, replied—" I can yet find words to thank you, sir; it is the most welcome news you could give me, what should I wish to live for?" Falling back with these expressions on his lips, he expired without further effort.

Thus ended a career of absolute unselfishness in a death which was, we trust, accepted by the Giver of Life as one of complete self-sacrifice.

Chapter XXIII.

THE BODENSTOWN CHURCHYARD.

In Bodenstown churchyard there is a green grave,
And wildly along it the winter winds rave:
Small shelter, I ween, are the ruined walls there,
When the storm sweeps down on the plains of Kildare.
                                                DAVIS.

THE patriot's body was given over to his relatives, and interred quietly in Bodenstown Churchyard. Thomas Davis visited the spot, when preparing to write his projected life of Tone early in the forties. His premature death prevented his carrying out that work of which he had written but a few pages and a dedication to the patriot's wife, then still living in the United States.

November 9th, 1861, brought other pilgrims to that "grave in green Kildare." A deputation had come across the broad Atlantic, bearing the body of Terence Bellew MacManus to be interred in Irish soil. November 10th was the day fixed for that eventful funeral, and on the day preceding it some members of the deputation from America stole away quietly from Dublin to look upon the grave of the great United Irish Leader, in whose steps they were one and all sworn to follow. Michael Cavanagh, the sole survivor of that little party of pilgrims, has favoured us with a description of the grave as it then was.

The little churchyard of Bodenstown is situated on the right of the road, going north from Sallins. As I sat on that side of the car I was the first of our party over the style. I remembered having read in "Madden's United Irishman" that Tone's grave was close by the south wall of the ruin in the centre of the churchyard, so in half a minute I reached it, and, before any of my companions had joined me, I was in possession of the only green thing that grew on the grave

—a plant of marsh-mallow. (I kept this much-prized relic for several years, until it crumbled into dust.)

When the rest of the pilgrims came up we stood for a moment silently reading the inscription prepared by Thomas Davis for the tombstone which himself and his friends had placed over what, until then, had been "a green grave." Then, moved by a common impulse, all knelt simultaneously and prayed for *his* soul who had brought "*a soul into Ireland.*"

Having reverentially honoured the memory of the dead hero, whose dust lay beneath that monumental slab, we contemplated more leisurely the grave and its surroundings.

Bodenstown churchyard is one of the smallest I have seen in Ireland, being not much more than an acre in extent.

Though very ancient, and, consequently, the burial place of countless generations, it contains but few monumental records, not more than a score of headstones being visible at the time of our visit. It is bounded on three sides by fertile fields, and on the fourth by the highroad.

The ruin in the centre of the churchyard is, like the enclosure, of very limited dimensions, the space inside its walls forming a rectangle of about fifty by twenty feet. Its walls seem considerably higher within than without, owing, no doubt, to the ground outside having been gradually raised by the numerous interments. The ruin was roofless and seemed bare of ornament, save the tufts of half-withered grass, and the clusters of dark green ivy that over-topped its weather-stained walls, and rustled mournfully in every passing breeze. I know not whether the building was originally a church or an abbey. Dr. Madden says it was an abbey; but, if he is correct, the community it harboured must not have been very numerous.

I observed, with a feeling of regret and indignation, that the interior of the venerable edifice had been evidently used as a "ball alley" by the boys of the vicinity; but consoled myself with the sage apophthegm—"Boys will be boys."

Tone's monument was *then* a heavy limestone slab, about six inches in thickness. It stood quite close to the centre of the south wall of the ruin. It was elevated about a foot from the ground, and rested on six stone supporters. It bore the following simple and suggestive inscription:—

> **THEOBALD WOLFE TONE,**
>
> *Born 20th of June, 1763.*
>
> *Died 19th of November, 1798,*
>
> **FOR IRELAND.**

In less than two years after the erection of this monumental stone, Thomas Davis was laid to rest in Mount Jerome. '48 saw most of his co-labourers scattered over the globe, and, for a long time thereafter, Bodenstown was but rarely visited by strangers. Consequently the "Martyr's Grave" received little attention, and that only when some local admirer, attending a funeral in the lonely little churchyard, went to draw hope and inspiration from the sacred spot.

At the time of our visit the ground beneath the tombstone was dry, hard, and bare; and, judging from the feathers scattered around it, had apparently become a favourite resort for domestic fowls.

But with the advent of Fenianism a reaction in national sentiment set in. It was manifested in various ways, but perhaps in no instance was it so strongly exhibited as in the devotion shown to the memory of Ireland's patriot dead. The lone grave in Bodenstown became again the resort of enthusiastic pilgrims. Few "Nationalists" visiting Dublin returned home without going to see it.

In the metropolis a permanent organisation, which was named after the "Martyr for Ireland," makes an annual pilgrimage, with music and banners, to where his dust reposes.

It is to be regretted that a sentiment so commendable in itself should lead to abuses that all right-minded patriots must condemn. Some over-zealous pilgrims, in their eagerness to possess mementoes of their visit to Bodenstown, have set the pernicious example of carrying off portions of the tomb itself.

Those pioneer iconoclasts unfortunately found so many imitators, that, in a few years, the original monument having become so much mutilated, the members of the "Dublin Wolfe Tone Band" deemed it advisable to have it replaced by a new one of a similar design. This was fenced in by a suitable iron railing erected by the "Men of Kildare," to protect it from future patriotic depredators.

We, too, felt desirous of possessing some mementoes of our pilgrimage, and, accordingly, I was deputed to cut, for each of my companions, a branch of ivy from that portion of the ruined wall immediately over the tomb. In addition to these, I went prospecting on the churchyard hedges until I found and cut a blackthorn stick, which I brought back to New York as a *souvenir* for John O'Mahony.

Appendix.

THE KINDRED AND DESCENDANTS OF TONE. GRAVES IN AMERICA.

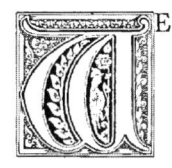

WE have already observed how the brothers and sister of Tone were, like himself, cut off in their prime, and, till recently, we were under the impression that not only his father's family, but his own descendants had died out.

Mr. Barry O'Brien's admirable edition of the patriot's life offered no further information on this point than that the widow and daughter of William Tone (sole surviving son of the patriot) were alive in America in the year 1858. As Tone's other children died of decline in Paris early in the century, and as William Tone succumbed to the same insidious complaint in his 28th year, one was inclined to assume that his orphan daughter had not long survived, and that there was no living descendant of the great patriot. How such extraordinary ignorance, on a matter in which the people of Ireland are vitally interested could have come about, it is hard to say. From Mrs. John Martin, the widow of a revered patriot and the sister of John Mitchel, we heard, for the first time, that the granddaughter of Wolfe Tone is living at this very day in the United States, and that as mother of seven children and grandmother of eight of another generation, she has handed down to a family, to which we wish prosperity and endurance "till the judgment," traditions prouder than those of any royal line of Europe. The papers, relics, and portraits of the great United Irishman are all safe in the keeping of this estimable family, every member of which is sensible of the honour which is their birthright.

To William Tone's biography of his father is appended

a most interesting and graphic account of the interview which the patriot's widow had with the great Napoleon. The result of that interview was that her eldest and sole surviving boy became a cadet in the Imperial School of Cavalry at St. Germains. In 1813 he became a sub-lieutenant in the 8th regiment of Chasseurs, and served in the battles of Lowenberg, Goldberg, Dresden, Bautzen, Muhlberg, Acken, and Leipzig. He received the Legion of Honour, but, on Napoleon's fall, was left without prospects at this crisis. The Mr. Wilson (referred to in Tone's last letters to his wife) crossed from America and married Mrs. Tone (then eighteen years a widow), in order to place his fortune at her disposal. They went to America, and resided in Georgetown, D.C., William Tone entering the United States Army. We are privileged to give the following brief summary of their fate and fortunes from an account kindly furnished to us by Miss Kate Maxwell, Tone's great-grand-daughter.

"Tone's son married the daughter of William Sampson, Counsellor-at-Law, who was banished in '98. In this country he (Sampson) and his fellow-exiles, Thomas Addis Emmett and William James MacNeven and their families, were always intimate. (Emmet's son and MacNeven's daughter, for instance, were my god-parents.) Tone's widow, who married in 1816 the faithful friend of Tone and herself, Thomas Wilson, went to live with him in Georgetown, D.C., now a part of Washington. Mr. Wilson died first in 1824, then my grandfather in 1828, and, finally, Matilda Tone Wilson in 1849.

They were buried in the Presbyterian burying-ground.

In 1891 this burying-ground was sold, and the Irish-American Union of Washington, which had always cared for and decorated the graves, guarded the remains until I came to remove them to my mother's lot in Greenwood Cemetery, Brooklyn. On the eve of All Saints' Day they were interred there with the remains of William Sampson, his wife, Grace

Clarke, and his daughter, Catherine Anne Tone, which had been removed from the family burying-ground on Long Island. The prayers of the Protestant Episcopal Church were said over them, and a wreath of ivy was laid on the new graves. The family of John Mitchell were present with us.

In the following Spring the monuments of stone, which had been also removed from Georgetown and Long Island, were again placed over their ashes.

Sampson's wife, Grace Clarke, and his only daughter, Catherine, who married Tone's son, were born in Belfast, also my own father, so we are greatly tied to that city, and I would gladly visit it. We have just seen a book on old Belfast, compiled by Robert Young, and printed by Marcus Ward. In it is a very interesting account of Mary Anne M'Cracken."

Referring to the fact that Belfast is sadly changed from the Nationalist town, which honoured Wolfe Tone, Miss Maxwell expresses her opinion that it is the result of ignorance of the past and sectarian differences, which she trusts will pass away. In conclusion, she informs us that her Maxwell ancestors came from Portaferry, County Down. The descendants of Theobald Wolfe Tone, therefore come of a good Ulster stock, a blend in pedigree, which would delight the Ulster-loving patriot.

Alluding to Mr. Barry O'Brien's splendid edition of Tone's life, she writes:—

"The arrangement suits the present times, and Mr. O'Brien's notes are a great addition." She, however, regrets the change of title. Of our own little venture, she kindly says:—

"I am glad to know you are preparing a short life of Wolfe Tone, which will be within the means of those who are poor in the world's goods, but rich in the qualities of the heart."

EPITAPHS ON THE GRAVES IN GREENWOOD CEMETERY.

In Memory of

M A T I L D A.

Widow by her second marriage of Thomas Wilson, born June, 1769, died March 18th, 1849,

Revered and loved as the heroic wife of Theobald Wolfe Tone.

Here lie the remains of

THOMAS WILSON.

Born in Edinburgh, Scotland, on the 25th of October, 1750, Died in Georgetown, D.C., on the 27th June, 1824.

His life was consecrated to works of benevolence, and his wishes and endeavours all tended to the happiness, information, and freedom of mankind.

In this grave lie the remains of

WILLIAM THEOBALD WOLFE TONE,

Last remaining son of the Martyred Irish Patriot, Theobald Wolfe Tone.

Born the 29th April, 1791, and departed this life the 11th October, 1828.

This stone is consecrated to his memory by his bereaved and inconsolable mother.

Sacred to the Memory of

CATHERINE ANNE TONE,

Wife of William Theobald Wolfe Tone and daughter of William Sampson.

Born September 1st, 1798, died December 17th, 1864.

Aged 66 years 3 months and 16 days.

In Memory of

GRACE SAMPSON,

Faithful wife and affectionate mother; an upright woman, an humble Christian.

Born in Belfast, Ireland, November 28th, 1764.
Died August 6th, 1855.

"I look for the Lord; my soul doth wait for Him; in His Word is my trust."

Beneath this stone lie the mortal remains of

WILLIAM SAMPSON.

Born in Londonderry, Ireland, January 27th, 1764.
Died in New York, December 28th, 1836.

An United Irishman, he defended the cause of civil and religious liberty. His countrymen requited his services by their love. His enemies attested his wisdom, and atoned for their persecution by adopting his measures. The cheerful temper and invincible fortitude that supported him in the dungeons of the Inquisition sustained him during his long exile and through his last, most painful sickness, and shed an affecting serenity round his departing spirit. He was resigned to the will, and trusted in the mercy of his God.

This stone is erected and inscribed to his memory by an affectionate wife and only daughter.

THE END.

BIBLIOLIFE

Old Books Deserve a New Life
www.bibliolife.com

Did you know that you can get most of our titles in our trademark **EasyScript**™ print format? **EasyScript**™ provides readers with a larger than average typeface, for a reading experience that's easier on the eyes.

Did you know that we have an ever-growing collection of books in many languages?

Order online:
www.bibliolife.com/store

Or to exclusively browse our **EasyScript**™ collection:
www.bibliogrande.com

At BiblioLife, we aim to make knowledge more accessible by making thousands of titles available to you – quickly and affordably.

Contact us:
BiblioLife
PO Box 21206
Charleston, SC 29413